"Full of wit, wisdom, grace, and humor, Dr. Larimore gives us a glimpse of the life of a small-town doctor. This is both an entertaining and delightful read. I can't recommend it highly enough."

Debbie Macomber, #1 *New York Times* bestselling author

Praise for *The Best Medicine*

"This book is more than fun homespun stories of small-town medicine. You may see yourself in its mirror, yet trust me, you'll be the better for it in the end."

Jerry B. Jenkins, *New York Times* bestselling
novelist and biographer

"Once again, Dr. Larimore has provided a delightful book full of sound wisdom and fascinating characters. Enjoy a great read!"

Ruth Graham, author of *Forgiving My Father, Forgiving Myself*

"With grace and humor, Dr. Walt Larimore delights the reader with an honest and heartwarming journey of discovery. From his early days as a young doctor, this memoir takes a poignant look at what it means to be a Christian physician, friend, husband, and father. *The Best Medicine* is an enjoyable view of life through Dr. Walt's compassionate eyes."

Jan Drexler, bestselling author of *Hannah's Choice*
(Journey to Pleasant Prairie series)

"Warm, inviting, and nostalgic. Dr. Walt Larimore brings to life a rich cast of characters and their Central Florida home in his tale of finding a fresh start and true healing."

Liz Johnson, bestselling author of *The Red Door Inn*

"Dr. Walt Larimore has written a delightful look at the life of a small-town doctor chock-full of interesting characters and medical tales. This is the kind of book you want to sip like sweet tea but wind up drinking in a satisfying gulp. You will enjoy the journey!"

Chris Fabry, Moody Radio host and author of *A Piece of the Moon*

"I was raised a small-town girl—one who moved from the low country of coastal Georgia to the 'big city' in Central Florida. *The Best Medicine* resonated with every fiber of my being. I have always enjoyed small-town, front-porch tales, and Dr. Walt Larimore's book fits the bill perfectly. I guarantee that when you read this collection of stories that reflect on his family's move from Bryson City, NC, to Kissimmee, FL, you'll laugh, you'll cry, you'll yearn for a simpler time—and you will desire to know the daily God, the God of our days, more intimately."

Eva Marie Everson, CBA #1 bestselling author, award-winning speaker, and president of Word Weavers International, Inc.

"After reading *The Best Medicine*, I could settle for calling author Walt Larimore an engaging storyteller. But he's more than that. Dr. Larimore connects with people through their stories and truly cares about their life experiences. In *The Best Medicine*, he shares a delightful assortment of stories with us in such a way that I felt as if I was sitting across the table from him, not reading a book. I laughed. I cried. And I found myself caring about people I've never met."

Beth K. Vogt, Christy Award–winning author of the Thatcher Sisters series

Praise for the Bryson City Series

"With homespun warmth, my friend Dr. Walt Larimore tells stories that integrate the science and art of medicine. Walt is a brilliant lifelong learner who is patient centered. *Bryson City Tales* portrays medical practice as something deeply personal, relational, and spiritual."

Randy Alcorn, bestselling author of *Deadline* and *The Treasure Principle*

"Walt Larimore has the gift. His fine book brings before the reader a vivid world inhabited by colorful people. We see the tragedy and triumph of their lives, and like a master, Doc Larimore employs the old show-business adage, 'Make 'em laugh—make 'em cry!' If you are seeking a book that delights and informs, you need look no further than *Bryson City Tales*."

Gilbert Morris, bestselling author of the House of Winslow series and the Appomattox series

"How does a young doctor manage to integrate his background of high academic medical training and simple Christian faith into the hurly-burly of established human relationships in a mountain community? This sounds like heavy stuff, but it turns out to be light—almost hilarious—reading."

Paul Brand, MD, bestselling coauthor (with Philip Yancey) of *Fearfully and Wonderfully Made* and *The Gift of Pain*

THE
Best Gift

THE

Best Gift

TALES OF A SMALL-TOWN DOCTOR
LEARNING LIFE'S GREATEST LESSONS

Walt Larimore, MD

Revell

a division of Baker Publishing Group
Grand Rapids, Michigan

Published by Revell
a division of Baker Publishing Group
PO Box 6287, Grand Rapids, MI 49516-6287
www.revellbooks.com

Printed in the United States of America

Library of Congress Cataloging-in-Publication Data
Names: Larimore, Walter L., author.
Title: The best gift : tales of a small-town doctor learning life's greatest lessons / Walter Larimore, MD.
Description: Grand Rapids, MI : Revell, a division of Baker Publishing Group, [2021]
Identifiers: LCCN 2021009416 | ISBN 9780800738235 (paperback) | ISBN 9780800741280 (casebound)
Subjects: LCSH: Larimore, Walter L. | Physicians—North Carolina—Kissimmee—Biography. | Medicine, Rural—Florida—Kissimmee—Anecdotes. | Family medicine—Florida—Kissimmee—Anecdotes.
Classification: LCC R154.L267 A3 2021 | DDC 610.92 [B]—dc23
LC record available at https://lccn.loc.gov/2021009416

21 22 23 24 25 26 27   7 6 5 4 3 2 1

Contents

9

Contents

Contents

To Barb, Kate, and Scott
Three of my bestest gifts ever!

In the medical profession, we do have a matchless, wonderful opportunity to meet people at times of their real need when they are ready to open up their hearts and expose their fears and worries and concerns. . . . They are broken and afraid when they face a medical situation . . . and this gives us the opportunity to present the grace of our Lord Jesus Christ.

Paul Wilson Brand, MD, OBE, medical missionary,
hand surgeon, and physician for lepers

[Jesus] sent them out to be preachers of the kingdom of God, and to make well those who were ill.[1]

The physician Luke, author of the largest
portion of the New Testament

Foreword

You're going to love every page of Walt Larimore's book *The Best Gift*. And before the last page, you're going fall in love with this wonderful doctor and his down-home wonderful sense of humor, from *"It's hot enough for our chicken to lay hard-boiled eggs"* to his description of life in a small town, *"If you don't know what you're doing, everyone else does!"* His charming tales about the patients who sought his help showcase his gentle spirit and his heart for God.

I promise you will smile when you read about Margie, the hypochondriac he won over with kindness and honesty. Or Leon the widower, who became a lost soul until Dr. Larimore stepped into his life. From one chapter to the next, Walt's charming tales of a small-town doctor will intrigue and bless you.

He is the physician we all want at our bedside. His caring, loving attitude toward his patients brings back times of yesteryear when medicine wasn't about the bottom line and government mandates.

I was fortunate to meet Walt several years ago while on a book tour. We were both being interviewed and struck up a conversation. He was warm and sincere, and I never forgot our chance encounter. I am fortunate to call him my friend.

Now sit back and enjoy this wonderful book. Don't be surprised if you read it in one sitting.

Debbie Macomber, #1 *New York Times* bestselling author

Introduction

Welcome to the fifth book about my journey as a young family physician, husband, and father. Here are some quick facts about me. I was born in Charlottesville, Virginia, where my father was finishing his master's degree. When I was sixteen months old, Dad moved us to Baton Rouge, Louisiana, where he began his doctoral studies at Louisiana State University.

I met my future wife, Barb, in kindergarten when we were five years old, and we finished high school and college together in Baton Rouge. We were married our last year of college and then headed to New Orleans where Barb taught middle school and I attended LSU School of Medicine. I was blessed to become involved with the Christian Medical Society and finished in the top five of my graduating class with AOA (Alpha Omega Alpha Honor Medical Society) Honors.

After medical school, I participated in the Queen's teaching fellowship in Nottingham, England. When that was completed, we moved to Durham, North Carolina, so I could attend the family medicine residency, with an emphasis in sports medicine at the Duke University Medical Center. Our first child, Katherine Lee, was born in Durham.

For private practice, we then moved to Bryson City in the Smoky Mountains, where I practiced with Rick Pyeritz, MD, for four years. That's also where our second child, Scott Bonham, was born.

This small town, with nine hundred citizens and over forty churches, became the source for three of my bestselling books—*Bryson City Tales*, *Bryson City Seasons*, and *Bryson City Secrets*.

Our young family walked through an extremely difficult experience that led us to relocate to a small town called Kissimmee in Central Florida, where I practiced family and sports medicine with John Hartman, MD, for fifteen years. I was privileged to serve as the president of the Florida Academy of Family Physicians and was named America's Outstanding Family Medicine Educator (the Thomas W. Johnson Award) by the American Academy of Family Physicians. While we lived in Kissimmee, Barb and I were honored to be named the Christian Medical Association's Educators of the Year.

During my "Florida years," besides practicing family medicine and delivering over 1,500 babies, I became a part-time medical journalist and hosted over 850 episodes of the daily, live *Ask the Family Doctor* show on Fox's Health Network, which was televised from Universal Studios in Orlando. I received the prestigious Gracie Award by the American Women in Radio and Television in 2000.

The first book about our family's early years in Kissimmee, *The Best Medicine*, came out in October 2020. What you now hold in your hands (or are reading on a screen) is the follow-up story. My prayer is that this book will be a joy and a blessing to you and your family.

PART ONE
Storms to Come

God allows myriad storms to
combat our arrogance.

Walt Larimore, MD

1

The Wreck

I WAS IN SCRUBS, driving the few minutes from home to the hospital in my old "trusty and dusty" pickup truck. It was the middle of a chilly, moonless night. Dr. Ken Byerly from the ER had paged me to come see a patient complaining of chest pain. As I skidded around a corner, I saw scores of flashing lights a few blocks ahead. I drove up to see if I might be able to help and parked behind two fire trucks, several police cars, and an ambulance.

On the other side of a deeply gouged residential front lawn, a police cruiser had crashed into an oak tree. Its front end was wrapped around the massive trunk, and the dashboard thrust back, trapping the motionless driver in a cab filled with smoke. A burning stench permeated the scene while steam hissed from the engine compartment, but there was no visible fire. The remnants of fire-suppressing foam covered the front of the car and the surrounding lawn. The noxious scent of burned rubber and oil contaminated the scene.

I walked over and recognized Kissimmee police chief Frank Ross standing close to the vehicle. "What in the world happened?" I asked.

"One of my men was on patrol. He must have fallen asleep. He's not in good shape and is pinned in."

"In North Carolina, I had medical rescue and extraction training. Happy to help."

"Just might need you."

Firefighters with hoses were at the front and back of the car, while two were positioning their Jaws of Life—a hydraulic tool used by emergency rescue personnel to assist in the extrication of a crash victim from their vehicle.

Frank commented, "Because the doors are jammed, the EMTs had to break the door window for access to stop the bleeding from an ugly head wound and splint what they think is a broken wrist. The wreckage has crushed and pinned his leg. They'll use the Jaws to open the doors. Dr. Pete Gonzales, who serves as the police department surgeon, is on his way. Y'all may have to amputate my officer's lower leg to get him out."

The metal squealed and creaked as the Jaws pried open the driver's door. The firefighters backed away, indicating to the chief it was safe. "You mind checking him out?" Frank asked me.

"Not at all. Who is it?"

"Gib. Gib Michaels."

We had frequently worked together. I rushed to the cruiser, crouched next to my friend, and found him unresponsive. His still-buckled seat belt held him upright. He had a cervical collar on his neck and a bloodied bandage around his forehead and scalp. Dried blood stained the front of his face and neck, while still-moist blood discolored the front of his uniform and pooled in his lap. I tried rousing him with no luck.

"Doc, when we checked a few minutes ago, his heart rate was 124, respirations 24, systolic 160," an EMT said from behind me. "Nasty forehead laceration—to the bone—but the bleeding stopped with direct pressure."

These numbers were elevated, likely due to pain. At least Gib's blood pressure wasn't low, which would indicate shock. "Got a bright light?"

The EMT handed me a small flashlight, which I used to check

Gib's eyes. "Pupils equal and respond briskly. But he's unresponsive. Severe concussion, at the very least—maybe worse." Gib had a wrist splint on his left arm, which I lifted to examine.

"Still got a pulse?" the EMT asked.

"Checking now."

I unhooked the Velcro and took off the brace. Gib's left wrist cocked up at a hideous angle. It was a fracture I had seen many times in folks who fall and land on the heel of their palm with the wrist extended. It's called a *FOOSH*—a Fall On Outstretched Hand–type fracture. Here, it was most likely from his extended hand hitting the steering wheel or dashboard during the crash. His palm and fingers were ice-cold. I tried to find an arterial pulse on either side of the wrist, but to my dismay there was none, meaning that there was no circulation going to his hand. I knew I had no choice but to reduce the fracture as quickly as possible. Otherwise, Gib could lose his hand. I had done these quite a few times in my brief career but never in this scenario.

The Jaws of Life fired up and pried the passenger side door open. Dr. Pete Gonzales, who also served as chief of staff at the hospital, crawled in. I explained my assessment and plan. "Do it!" he instructed. "By the way, I just came from the ER. Dr. Byerly said your patient with chest pain is stable and in the ICU. No rush to go see him."

I chuckled. "Well, that's good news!" I grasped Gib's left forearm with my right hand and then grabbed his left hand with my left hand as if we were shaking hands. I then pulled my hands apart while extending his wrist to unlock the compressed ends of the large forearm bone—the radius. Then, while pulling as hard as I could, I flexed the wrist while everting it outward. The bones crunched against each other as Gib yelled in pain, but the reduction worked and the deformity disappeared. "His pulse is back!" I exclaimed to Pete. "His hand is warming up."

"Outstanding job!" Pete said as Gib moaned. "That may have been what we needed to wake up our officer."

I replaced the wrist splint. "Gib!" I yelled, gently slapping his cheek. "Officer Michaels!"

"Quit yelling at me!" he responded. "I can hear you. What happened?"

He had no recollection of the entire evening. It's what we call *retrograde amnesia*, a sure sign of a traumatic brain injury in which one loses short-term but usually not long-term memory—as was evident with his next statement. "Are you the doctor with the ugly truck?"

"Guilty," I said, as Pete and I both chuckled. "It's not fifty feet from us now."

"Better watch out, Doc," Gib said. "Chief Ross is likely to have that fool thing towed off!" He chuckled and groaned at the same time. It was great to see him try to smile.

"Let's see if we can get him out," Pete said. "I've done more than my share of these types of extractions on the highways around here." He shined a flashlight into the mangled wreckage at Gib's feet. "Looks like the wreckage has crushed and lacerated his right lower leg."

Pete turned to the EMTs outside the car and requested leather gloves for each of us. With them on, we contorted ourselves into position to explore the twisted metal, rubber, and interior upholstery that had trapped Gib's leg. To our surprise, I was able to squeeze my hands down and around his lower leg and foot and protect it as Pete pulled back enough debris to free the leg. Unfortunately, it began hemorrhaging.

"Hold direct pressure!" Pete ordered. As I did, my stomach sickened when I felt the splintered ends of Gib's tibia and fibula sticking out through the skin.

Pete turned and yelled, "Tourniquet! Stat!" An EMT handed him one, and he placed it below Gib's knee and cinched it up. "Let go of the pressure, Walt." I did, and the bleeding did not start back up.

"Walt, you secure the leg. I will let the boys get in here and cut him out of his seat belt. Then we'll extract him from this side, and you follow. But keep pulling to distract the bones. That will help pull them back and set them."

"I suspect this will hurt!" Gib predicted.

"Like the dickens!" I said.

"Can I get a pain shot before you do any more?"

"I'd love to, Officer," Pete answered, "but we have to have you awake. We may need your help."

Just then someone outside yelled, "Fire!" I looked up to see flames in the engine compartment. I barely had time to clench my eyes shut and duck my head as a fireball rocked the car.

2

The Prayer

PETE DUCKED WITH HIS GLOVED HANDS over his head, while I grabbed a deep breath, held it, jerked backwards, and spun to cover Gib as I threw my arms around him. The flames crackled, and every fiber of my being was screaming to flee the intense blaze that filled the driver's compartment. The skin and hair on the back of my scalp and neck singed. The temptation to bolt was overwhelming. I prayed silently, *Father, protect us!*

Just in the nick of time, the firefighters on either side of the car, whose training prepared them for such situations, opened their hoses. The flames hissed and disappeared, and the forceful inundation suppressed the fire in seconds. It soaked the three of us to the skin; however, the cold liquid was a lifesaver and felt exquisite.

"Walt, I'm backing out!" Pete yelled as he crawled backward.

"You okay?" I said to Gib.

He nodded.

A firefighter replaced Pete. "Skedaddle, Doc!"

"I'm staying!"

"Suit yourself!" His knife sliced off Gib's seat belt. I could still feel the heat of the metal behind me. Out of the corner of my eye,

I could see more flames erupting from the engine. A voice behind me bellowed, "Get another hose over here. Now!"

"Doc," Gib said as I looked into his eyes. "It's okay to leave. Get on out. Save yourself."

"I'm not leaving without you, Officer."

He smiled as tears spilled down his cheeks. The compartment was again filling with smoke and steam. Gib and I coughed, and our eyes watered. A firefighter wiggled into the police cruiser from the passenger side to help wrestle Gib out. I extracted his leg from its trap as the man began to pull him out. I resisted the tugging so as to apply traction on Gib's foot and ankle. It pleased me when the bones sucked back into the wound and crunched together.

The firefighters extricated Gib and laid him on a gurney. One EMT hooked him up to an oxygen mask, while another checked his vital signs. A third began covering his wounds as Pete expertly placed a pressure dressing on his leg and then carefully loosened the tourniquet.

"Superb job with the reduction, Walt," Pete said.

As they worked, I held Gib's hand and asked him questions, partially to test his cognition, partially to keep him awake. Chief Ross was on the other side, holding Gib's other hand, and I could see the mist in his eyes. Over time, I learned that this seasoned public servant had a soft heart for each of his officers and their families.

I knew what I wanted to do next, but could I? With so many people around? The more cautious part of me went into attack mode, warning me, *Don't do it! Or if you do, it will be at your peril!* My thoughtful inside voice came to my defense, *It's never wrong to do what's right*, adding, *This is a life-and-death emergency!*

"You a praying man?" I asked Gib.

"I am tonight, Doc!"

"Could I offer a quick prayer of thanks and for healing?"

He nodded. "I'd appreciate that."

Just then, a familiar person strode up. It was Pastor Pete Zieg from the Lutheran church. He served as the chaplain for the fire department. He greeted Gib—they knew each other—and looked up at me. "Are *you* a praying man, Doc?" Pastor Pete asked.

"I am, Pastor, but will yield to the professional."

Pete smiled and glanced at the EMTs. "Gentlemen, do we have time for a very brief prayer?"

"*Very* brief!" one answered.

"That's how we Lutherans do it," Pete said, laughing.

Everyone chuckled. Pete prayed thanksgiving for the first responders who saved Gib, asked God for healing and recovery for him and for wisdom for his medical team . . . "in Jesus's name!"

During the prayer, I had sneaked a peek to judge the response of the men. *How did they see this?* I wondered. *An intrusion? Proselytizing? Ministry?* The answer was apparent. Every man's head bowed; some were on their knees, while others' hands were outstretched toward Gib while joining Pastor Pete in a prayer of blessing.

"Amen!" Pete finished. "Let's go!"

"One favor?" Gib said to the EMTs.

"Yes, sir. What's that?"

"Please take me in your ambulance and *not* in Doc's truck!"

"I wouldn't put *me* in Doc's truck, much less you, Officer!" the beaming EMT declared.

There were chuckles all around as the EMTs rushed off with Gib. As we watched the ambulance drive away, lights flashing and siren screaming, Pastor Pete looked at my pickup and then at Dr. Gonzales. "Can't you convince him to get a more professional vehicle?"

The surgeon smiled and patted the cleric on his back as they walked away. "Lord knows I've tried, Pastor."

I cherished that old truck. It had been my dad's, and I would drive it for all the years I practiced in what was now my family's hometown. Part of the reason was an ornery streak. I didn't like the way vehicle salesfolk pulled every emotional string they could to sell you something new and shiny.

Another part of me was practical. My pickup was inexpensive to operate and even cheaper to maintain and repair—it was so easy that even I could do most of the work on it. My colleagues, staff, and friends all stifled giggles whenever they saw that the gun rack in my rear window held a large golf umbrella for protection against afternoon monsoons.

My kids, Kate and Scott, learned to drive in that trusty rust bucket on country roads and through fields and forests. We didn't have to worry about scratching or denting it, which gave us a lot of freedom to have fun. And having time with my children was important to me. When Scott, as a teenager, drove that junker around town, everyone knew it was him. No one else had an uglier or more practical truck. Scott couldn't go anywhere without being recognized. I'd like to think it kept him out of a lot of temptation and trouble. I made hospital, nursing home, and ranch and home visits in that truck. I loved it.

A year after Gib's accident, I received an invitation to the opening and dedication of the brand-spanking-new Kissimmee Police Headquarters. Since I had forgotten to bring my invite, the rookie officer assigned to the VIP parking lot didn't want to admit me—well, I guess he didn't want to let in that old truck. Then who should walk up but Gib Michaels. He still limped but over the months had made a miraculous recovery. Chief Ross bent over backward to give Gib all the time and resources he needed for extensive rehabilitation. When he was ready to return to the force, Frank eased Gib into his day-to-day duties.

"This man is *my* family physician," Gib said, laughing at the incredulous look of the freshly minted patrolman.

"*You* are a doctor?" the inexperienced officer asked. "Driving *that*?"

"The man spent an entire night with Dr. Gonzales in the operating room, patching me back together. Took care of me through my hospitalization and several months of rehab. Been with me every limp of the way," Gib explained, smiling at his pun. "Doc's an honored guest, no matter what he drives!"

"My apologies, sir," the youthful patrolman stammered.

Gib leaned toward me. "But you better watch out, Doc. Chief still doesn't like your old rust bucket. He says it's unbecoming. And you *are* the only physician that drives a truck." It was great to see him smile after a year of so much suffering.

When I left the ceremony, I noticed a card on my windshield—one of Chief Ross's business cards. I turned it over and chuckled as I read it:

The Police Dept. received a complaint about a junky brown truck reflecting negatively on this new complex. Requests the truck be towed. Please donate to the Salvation Army.

Frank R.

Every time I read the card, I laugh and am awash with warm and wonderful memories—even though it's been over three and a half decades since that day. That truck endeared me to the locals. Maybe it helped me become accepted sooner than I would have otherwise.

I remember my last day making rounds at the hospital before moving to Colorado a decade and a half later. As I jumped into that old truck, I noticed that about 80 percent of the vehicles in the physicians' parking lot were pickup trucks.

What had been anathema and even abomination was fashionable. Who would have thought it? Now the doctors' preferred vehicles were *very expensive pickups*. Nevertheless, my old truck allowed me to reflect on just how very much my family, that community, and I had changed. Although we had traveled some awfully bumpy roads before we got there!

3

It's Hot Here

AFTER FOUR YEARS of practice in Bryson City, North Carolina, on the southern border of Great Smoky Mountains National Park, my young family moved to Kissimmee in Central Florida, where we lived in a small ranch home as John Hartman, MD, and I built our family medicine practice.

Kissimmee's historic downtown was located on the northwestern shore of Lake Tohopekaliga, the seventh largest lake in Florida. Most of the locals called it Lake Toho. John, his wife, Cleta, and their three girls moved to Kissimmee three years earlier and purchased one of the few houses on the shore of Lake Toho. These heirloom homes, some of them over fifty years old, infrequently appeared on the market. After a patient of mine mentioned that hers was going up for sale as she was looking to downsize, Barb, my wife, and I visited with her. Only three doors down from the Hartmans' home, it turned out that this patient's gorgeous lakeside home, with its large southern live oak trees providing ample shade on three acres, was ideal for us. We quickly sold our first home while completing the appraisals, inspections, and legal agreements on the lakeside home in record time. We were convinced it would be our forever home; however, it needed some minor renovations. Our contractor estimated the face-lift would take several weeks, so we moved into a rental house in a neighborhood just across the street.

John and Cleta introduced us to our new next-door neighbors, Bill and Polly Prather. Bill, like many locals, was a descendant of Florida pioneers. Being a retiree and part-time travel agent allowed him to cultivate relationships with novice bird-watchers like me. We would often "bird" together on Saturdays. I rarely talked because Bill had so much to say. His knowledge of birds, Florida history, the cattle industry, church history, and myriad other topics was legendary, as was his wry sense of humor.

One scorching midsummer day, Bill and I drove to the ranch owned by Geech and Connie Partin. They were patients in our practice and had given Bill and me permission to walk the property whenever we desired. Their driveway was one mile of dirt road. The earthy, damp fragrance of the countryside permeated the heavy, humid air as we drove by lush pastures occupied by grazing Brahman and Angus cattle. We parked in front of their small brick home.

After a few hours of hiking and bird-watching, we arrived back at the car. Geech and Connie came out to greet us. Geech's round face was tan and creased by years of sun and weather. He was short, stocky, and well-muscled, with fingers twisted and ravaged by arthritis and many cowboying fractures. Connie's silver hair crowned a thin face, wrinkled from ranch living, but with a radiant smile that expressed welcome. She carried a tray with a pitcher of cold tea and glasses. "Won't you two have a seat and join us a bit?"

"How could we say no?" Bill exclaimed.

"It's a sweltering day, ain't it?" Geech said, putting his iced glass up to his forehead as we all sat under the shade of a tree. "It's hotter than blue blazes. Why, I believe it's hot enough to fry eggs on the sidewalk or for our chickens to lay some hard-boiled eggs."

"Here in Osceola County," Bill said, "there are only two seasons: summer's here or summer's coming."

Geech laughed. "I've always said, 'There's only two seasons around here: January and summer!'"

A large bull ambled up to the fence a few yards behind us and bellowed. "Doc, you remember Wrinkles," Geech boasted. "You've met him on trips out here." He turned to Bill. "He's my favorite, and he knows it. Weighs almost two tons, but he's just a big, blubbering baby. He follows me around the pastures like a puppy." Geech laughed. How I loved his laughter, which came easily for him. We finished our tea and said our goodbyes. However, when I opened the car door, it felt like I was opening an oven door with the heating element turned up high.

"This car is so hot, I'm sweating like a politician on election day," Bill commented as he turned the air on high. We had to wait a moment for the "cool" air to blow in before we could head home.

Once we were moving, I commented on the temperature. "I can't imagine living here without air-conditioning!"

"You're not the only one to complain about living here. I've read about Spanish soldiers stationed down here in the early 1800s calling Florida a hideous, loathsome, diabolical, God-abandoned mosquito refuge. Those were their actual words!"

Bill laughed. "Even the future US president Zachary Taylor, who commanded troops down here for two years, said that he wouldn't trade a square foot of Michigan or Ohio for a square mile of Florida."

I chuckled. "Sounds like the Sunshine State wasn't very popular with early settlers."

"You're right. It's easy to forget that Central and South Florida were once America's last frontier. Settlements down here didn't even begin until well after we won the West. In the 1880s, the numbers of hearty pioneers in Central Florida were only in the hundreds. One visitor said if he owned land here and in hell, he would rent the property here to someone else and live in hell."

"What brought folks to this area?" I asked.

"An industrialist from Philadelphia, Hamilton Disston, bought four million acres of Central Florida from the State of Florida in 1881 for twenty-five cents an acre. He began dredging canals, waterways, and draining the swamplands. His headquarters was in a small pioneer settlement on the shores of Lake Toho called Allendale. In 1884 Allendale incorporated as Kissimmee City and developed into a hub of commerce and trade."

"What type of industry? Allendale had to be some kind of backwater place back then."

"Literally!" Bill said, laughing. "The town became the home port for steamboats plying the Kissimmee River from Lake Toho south to Lake Okeechobee, which some call Florida's Inland Sea. But it was the railroad that took Kissimmee to another level. The first one connected Kissimmee to Tampa and Jacksonville. The lumber and cattle industry exploded. By 1890, the population of Kissimmee had ballooned up to almost 2,500 folks."

"Cattle are still big here. How long did the lumber industry last?"

Bill shook his head. "Not long. And with the loss of lumber, the population shrank to less than a thousand. After World War II, the city's focus shifted to tourism. Then in 1971, Disney World spurred growth here in Kissimmee to the 15,000 we have today."

"Has the growth been good?"

Bill thought before answering. "Locals learn to put up with the heat, humidity, mosquitoes, snakes, alligators, and bugs, but the worst varmints for most of us are the growing swarms of tourists. Though for me, the most significant positive is the folks that live here. Down-to-earth, as honest as the day is long. They would do about anything for you. Living here my whole life has given me lasting memories of a little town where people have a lot of fondness and respect for each other."

We pulled up to my rental house. "You say that I'll get used to this weather, Bill, and maybe so, but I'm not so sure. Anyway, we've fallen in love with the people here in Kissimmee. I can't imagine ever leaving."

"I don't think anyone should underplay the importance of living where people are kind, caring, and compassionate. That's what makes a place a community, not just a town. And Kissimmee still has that in spades."

I nodded and thanked him for a morning of terrific birding and his review of local lore and legends. But most of all, I cherished his giving me a fresh appreciation of our new hometown—one in which I hoped my family might one day be considered "locals" and not "outsiders."[1]

4

First Prayer Ever

DR. JOHN HARTMAN AND I loved caring for patients from conception. Pregnancy care and attending the birth of a newborn were unique joys for us. So, when several members of First Baptist Church of Kissimmee, which started in 1882, wanted to begin a ministry for young women experiencing unexpected pregnancies, we could not have been more supportive of the new outreach.

We were invited to lunch with the director of the newly established Osceola Pregnancy Center, Dawn Pate, who surprised us when she explained, "The organized American pro-life movement is over a hundred years old. As are our provision of crisis pregnancy centers, or what we call CPCs."

"Gosh," John said, "I thought CPCs started maybe twenty years ago."

"That's true for the modern CPC movement," she said. "It ramped up in the late '60s in the US and Canada. But between the end of the Civil War and the turn of the twentieth century, leading protectors of women and their unborn children included the Women's Christian Temperance Union, the YMCA and YWCA, the Florence Crittenton Society, and the Salvation Army. By the 1880s, hundreds of CPCs were scattered throughout major American cities, working hand in hand with what they called 'shepherding homes for unwed mothers.' Some of these ministries had room for more than a thousand girls to live at one time. Back then, the slogan 'Adoption, not Abortion' was wildly popular."

We couldn't have been happier to join hands with them and to attend church the day they announced the ministry to the congregation. Coincidentally, it was youth pastor Tim Wilder's first day on staff. He was a Florida native who finished seminary in Fort Worth before being called into youth ministry. It was the first of many services in which he would welcome folks and give the announcements. No one will forget what he did that day.

"Ladies and gentlemen," he began, "it delights my wife, Nancy, and me to serve you and your children. But—"

Tim turned to the senior pastor, Harold C. Epperson, who had led the congregation for twelve years and was the church's twenty-sixth pastor. "Before I deliver my first congregational prayer ever, I need to come clean and confess something." The crowd hushed; all eyes were on the young pastor. "I have to let you, the deacons, and the members know that I have a spiritual gift not given to most Baptists and rarely displayed in front of Southern Baptists."

He paused, and we could see Pastor Epperson shifting uncomfortably in his seat.

"What could it be?" Barb whispered. "Is he going to speak in tongues or something?"

Tim turned back to the apprehensive crowd and continued. "I should have told you all about this before I came, and I apologize for that. But you need to know the truth. So here we go."

He reached down and pulled out a glass of water, turned sideways to the congregation, and began to drink slowly. As he did,

Tim's recorded voice giving the day's announcements came over the speaker system. At first, there were chuckles, and then the laughter grew in a crescendo. In the end, he turned and said, "So my spiritual gift is to be able to give announcements as a ventriloquist while drinking." We and everyone there fell in love with Tim and his unique sense of humor that day. Tim went on to become the senior pastor and continues ministering there today.

Ron Smith and Ellen Jeffries were living together, but the last thing they wanted as an unmarried couple was a baby. When Ellen missed a menstrual period, she didn't tell Ron. She even kept her morning nausea a secret. But after missing her third period and developing a little belly pooch, she finally broke down and confessed. He didn't get angry or threaten to leave her, which she feared he might. Instead, he held her close.

"If you're pregnant," he said, "then we're in this together. But I'm not sure we can afford a baby, and I'm not sure we're ready to be parents. Maybe we should consider abortion and wait to have a baby when we're better prepared."

Ellen began to cry.

"What's the matter?" Ron asked.

"I'm scared that I'm too far along."

Ron had grown up in church, although he and Ellen never attended a service together. "Maybe we can go to that new pregnancy center and at least find out what our options are."

They showed up, unannounced, at the pregnancy center. One of the staff took their history and did a pregnancy test, which was positive. "Our ultrasound nurse is here today," the staff member said. "How about we take a look?"

"I don't know if we have the cash to cover that," Ron said.

"All of our services are complimentary."

Ellen began to drink water to fill her bladder as the nurse

examined her tummy. Once the ultrasound began, the baby's heartbeat sounded loud and clear. Ron and Ellen smiled at each other.

"That's our baby," Ellen said, holding Ron's hand.

The black-and-white image was hard to comprehend at first, but as the nurse explained what was on the screen, their eyes widened as they recognized the baby's hands, feet, face, and tiny organs, including the heart, lungs, stomach, and kidneys.

"Do you want to know your baby's sex?"

They both nodded, and the nurse moved the transducer around until she was able to offer a peek between the tiny baby's legs.

"Is that a . . . ?" Ron stammered.

"Yes," the nurse said, giggling. "That's your little guy's private part."

Ellen laughed as tears spilled down her cheeks, and they hugged.

After the ultrasound, the nurse explained how John and I would provide their prenatal care and delivery at no cost. If they wanted to keep the baby, the center would provide the support and supplies the young couple would need to prepare. If they wanted to give the baby up for adoption, the center would help them with all the costs and details.

In those early years of the CPC, we learned how very unusual it was for a mother or a couple, even those leaning strongly toward an abortion, to go through with it after seeing their baby on ultrasound. What was inside the mother was no longer an impersonal "clump of cells." No longer just an "it" but a living baby. Her baby—or in this case, *their* baby!

"I'm so excited it's a boy!" Ron exclaimed. Then his countenance fell. "But we just don't have much. We'll need all the help we can get."

"As I said, you'll have it!" the nurse replied. "We'll be sure of that. And besides physical care, you'll have access to emotional and spiritual care, plus marital and parenting resources will be available to you as well, if you want it."

Both smiled and nodded. It was far more than they could have hoped for.

"Can we start with a prayer for all three of you?"

The young couple nodded again and joined the nurse, Dawn, and another staff member for the first prayer ever for themselves and their boy.

5

Expect the Unexpected

ABOUT FOUR MONTHS LATER, Ron and Ellen's little boy, whom they had decided to name Timothy, was thirty-seven weeks' gestation—just three weeks from his due date. All was normal except that he was in the frank breech position—meaning he was in the pike position, with his legs stretched up, feet near his head, leaving his buttocks down next to the cervix.

I explained to Ron and Ellen that during my training at Duke and my first practice in Bryson City, I attended a number of vaginal breech deliveries and all turned out great. "However," I explained, "studies are now showing that breech babies born vaginally have a higher risk of harm compared to those delivered by C-section, especially the firstborn."

"Why?" Ellen asked.

"Since the largest part of a baby is the head, if the baby's narrower hips pass through the cervix first, it may not completely dilate. Your little guy's head can then be trapped by the incompletely dilated cervix and compress the umbilical cord. This could shut off Timothy's oxygen supply, which could result in brain damage or death."

"What can we do?" Ron asked.

Ellen's eyes widened, and she looked worried. "C-section?"

"I have another option you can consider," I told them. "I can arrange for an elective admission to the maternity care unit to attempt an external cephalic version. It's a procedure done under ultrasound guidance with electronic monitoring to follow your baby's heartbeat. I would have you in a birthing bed, with your head lowered a bit. This allows gravity to pull Timothy's bottom away from the cervix. Then I'll apply gentle pressure to his head with one hand and his buttocks with the other to front-flip him from butt first to headfirst."

"How often does it work?" Ellen asked.

"Success for versions is the highest when done at thirty-six to thirty-seven weeks because the baby is smaller than at term, and there's far more fluid around the baby. Also, at this point in a pregnancy, the baby can do very well out of the womb, which is important because, in the unlikely case of a problem during the procedure, such as a torn placenta or the umbilical cord wrapping around him, an immediate C-section can be done. However, if the procedure is successful, a much safer, natural, headfirst delivery can occur when you go into labor."

They decided to go for the external cephalic version instead of the C-section.

The morning of the procedure, Sandi Lynch, RN, one of our labor and delivery nurses, and our consultant obstetrician, Allan Pratt, DO, joined me on Ron and Ellen's birthing team. The C-section room was prepared and ready if needed. After Ron and Ellen signed all the proper forms, we gathered around to share a prayer for safety.

With my first attempt, the baby easily flipped. There were smiles and sighs of relief all around—until suddenly and entirely un-expectedly, the baby's heartbeat, which had been a typical 120 to

130 beats per minute, precipitously plummeted. Sandi immediately lowered Ellen's head even more while I did a rapid ultrasound. The placenta looked normal. But the heart rate kept dropping. It went from 80 and then down to 60 beats per minute. I could feel the perspiration beading on my forehead. I looked at Allan, who calmly said, "I'll stat scrub my hands." It was his way of telling me he was preparing for emergency surgery. "Why don't you try flipping the baby breech?"

I nodded, and he took off.

"Ron and Ellen," I said, turning to the parents-to-be, "something's compressing the baby's umbilical cord. So I'll try to reverse the version. If this does not work, we need to do a stat C-section. Okay?"

Both nodded as Ron grasped Ellen's hand. I gave a slow but steady push, but the baby wouldn't budge. I looked at the frightened couple. "We've got to get Timothy out ASAP."

"How much time do we have?" Ron asked.

"Minutes, Ron, only minutes. But don't worry. Our team handles emergencies like this all the time. If it's okay, it would be better for us if you would wait outside the OR in the waiting room." Ron quickly kissed and hugged Ellen and turned to leave.

After a quick scrub, Sandi and I joined Allan beside Ellen. We had done emergency C-sections together, and we knew we could get the little boy out quickly and safely. Then I would take him to the resuscitation table. The anesthesiologist, who had been on standby, quickly put Ellen to sleep. Nurses from the nursery set up the warmer to receive the baby and lay out the emergency equipment I might need. Allan and I prepped and draped Ellen's abdomen while a nurse placed a bladder catheter.

"Fetal heart at 30 to 40 beats per minute," another nurse said.

I knew we had only minutes to go before the risk of permanent brain damage would skyrocket.

"Vertical incision?" I asked Allan, who nodded. We preferred a transverse skin cut for most patients, called a *bikini* or *Pfannenstiel incision.* It had the best cosmetic appearance and less postoperative pain and risk of hernia formation than the vertical midline skin incision. The latter approach, however, would give us a reduced incision-to-delivery time that the baby desperately needed.

"Ready?" Allan asked the anesthesiologist.

"Go!" she said.

Allan made a rapid incision from the belly button to just above the pubic bone, through the skin and subcutaneous tissues to the fascia overlying the rectus muscle. He made a small transverse incision in the fascia, put the scalpel down, and we both inserted a finger under our side of the muscles and pulled them apart in unison. Allan bluntly opened the peritoneum, the lining of the abdominal cavity. It had taken only seconds, but we could see the glistening enlarged uterus. It looked healthy.

"Heart rate down to 20 beats per minute!" cried a nurse.

Sandi gave me an instrument called the *bladder blade*, and I inserted it to protect the bladder from damage while she handed Allan a fresh scalpel that he used to make a small incision in and through the wall of the uterus. There was a gush of clear, healthy amniotic fluid.

"No meconium!" Allan exclaimed. That was good news. A stressed baby can have its first bowel movement, which is greenish-brown and called *meconium*, inside the uterus. If inhaled by the baby, it can cause acute respiratory distress. At least we wouldn't have *that* to worry about.

Allan took bandage scissors and extended the incision. Handing the scissors back to Sandi, he pulled the wound apart, inserted his hand into the uterus, and quickly pulled the baby out.

I grabbed a suction bulb and began suctioning the infant's nose and mouth while Allan examined the umbilical cord. "It's wrapped around the body!" he said, confirming our suspicions. He clamped and cut it, then cried, "Go!"

I rushed with the baby to the waiting resuscitation warmer and team. Two nursery nurses stimulated him with warm towels. His eyes widened, but he didn't breathe. Again, I took the suction bulb and rapidly suctioned his nose and the back of his throat.

One nurse continued to stimulate Timothy by slapping the bottom of his feet as the other prepared for a possible cardiopulmonary resuscitation—CPR. I silently prayed. The next seconds seemed an eternity until the baby gasped, sneezed, took in his first deep breath, and then let out the most heaven-sent bellow. He quickly turned from a foreboding dark blue to beautiful pink as his respiratory rate, heart rate, and oxygen levels returned to normal.

Leaning over the tiny guy, who was lustily bawling, I said, "Well come, Timothy!" I took in a deep breath and let out a quick prayer of thanksgiving that we had saved the little guy's life.

"Well come!" was my standard greeting to every one of the over 1,500 babies I delivered in my medical career.[1] The vast majority of the births I attended over twenty years turned out well, even when emergencies like this suddenly popped up.

Yet birth care is almost always a journey into the unexpected. Usually the passage, like this one, ends in joy. When it came to labor and delivery and what to expect when our patients were expecting, however, it was always wise for us to expect the unexpected and to be prepared to respond. As one of my professors taught, "If you do not expect the unexpected, you will not find it or know how to handle it. Never forget that in labor and delivery, at least two lives are on the line."

Our L and D staff and I had been well-trained to keep a careful eye out for the unforeseen, unanticipated, and unpredicted birthing emergency and then to handle whatever raised its ugly head quickly and safely. Nevertheless, these startling events always raised my heart rate, apprehension, and *pucker factor*—a military slang phrase used to describe the level of stress in a pressure situation that my father, a World War II vet, liked to use.

But as I was compelled to learn during those early years of my career, marriage, and parenting journeys, there would be unforeseen surprises, storms, and suffering. I grew to expect unexpected disorder, disease, and even death as a natural part of the journey of life into which each of us is called.

6

Discipler

BILL JUDGE WAS A SECOND-GENERATION Florida dairyman and had been my mentor since I arrived in Kissimmee. We'd share breakfast at Joanie's Diner in historic downtown Kissimmee every Tuesday morning before I made rounds at the hospital. He served as my coach for my spiritual, professional, marital, and parenting roles in life. As an accomplished businessman, experienced family man, and deeply rooted man of faith who served as a church elder, his thoughtful wisdom and practical counsel were a continual blessing. In his profession, he was a milker of cows. But his gifting was as a fisher of men who molded followers of Jesus—he was a disciple maker par excellence.

"Tuesdays with Bill," I said as I scooted into the booth at Joanie's one morning. "An inexperienced physician learns life's greatest lessons from a master."

Bill laughed. "Sounds like a great title of a book, Walt. Would it be fiction?"

"It would be fun to write, as if I'll ever have any time to do any writing. Life's pretty full right now with the practice and the family. How are you doing?"

"If I were doing any better, they'd have to declare it a crime." Bill chuckled.

After ordering our breakfasts, I shared an update on our new house and my feeling a bit ashamed for not having had the faith that God was in charge of the details of our move. "Walt," Bill said, "I believe it's God who gives us the gift of faith. As we grow in our relationship with him, I think he just wants us to look to him. He's not only the founder of our faith but he's the perfecter of our faith too. It's not about what you do but what he does in and through you."

"That's great advice," I said as our food arrived.

"What I have found, and a lot of people don't like to hear this, is God chooses to cause or allow all sorts of troubles and trials for the specific purpose of growing our faith. The Bible says that 'anyone who wants to live all out for Christ is in for a lot of trouble; there's no getting around it.'"[1]

I took in a deep breath and slowly let it out. "Well, I've got to tell you, I wish there were an easier way to grow."

"Remember the story about Job in the Old Testament? He was a righteous man, but God allowed Satan to subject him to severe trials and afflictions. Job lost all of his property, his children died, and he suffered great physical agony. In the midst of all this, his friends accused him of doing evil and abandoning God. But Job chose to trust God during those awful storms and actually said, 'When he has tested me, I will come forth as gold.'"[2]

"I think I know what you mean," I said. "We've had some hard times with Kate's cerebral palsy diagnosis, which almost destroyed my faith and marriage."

"What saw you through?"

I thought as I stirred creamer into my coffee. "I think there were three key factors for my growth as a Christian. Comfort and guidance from God's Spirit, God's Word, the Bible, and God's people—other men and women of faith who have walked with us through some pretty dark chapters in our life."

"That's good. And I think those three perfect gifts in a Christian's life allow them to prepare for storms yet to come. Peter wrote that we shouldn't be surprised at fiery trials when they occur, that we shouldn't consider them strange or unusual."[3]

"I'm finding in my practice that most people are absolutely shocked when a disease or disorder hits. They assume it will never happen to them."

I took a sip of my coffee as Bill responded. "My experience is the same. I've found folks that are not astonished or perplexed when life's snags or struggles hit share three characteristics. Number one, they are aware that life, every life, will have storms. Guaranteed. They are going to happen. After all, Jesus told us that in this world, we would *all* have storms and trials and difficulties. It's part of life.

"Number two, these folks are prepared for disruptions and disturbances. They trust in the Lord, but they prepare. On the farm, we have an old saying. 'Pray as if everything depended on God, then work as if everything depended on you.' A pastor once preached, 'Remember, if you fail to prepare, you are preparing to fail.'[4] The Bible tells us to keep watch[5] and to keep alert at all times."[6]

Bill took a sip of juice and finished his mini sermon. "Finally, people that are not flummoxed by storms understand that they all will stop."

I chuckled. "As we say in medicine, 'All bleeding stops.'"

"On the farm, we say, all storms will end with a rainbow. Every time Jane and I gaze at a rainbow and its amazing beauty, we remember how God moved during every storm in our lives. No storm is complete without a rainbow."

"That's a great way of looking at things, Bill."

"Here's a verse that's been helpful for me during some of my life's storms, and it's from the book of James." He grabbed his Bible off the table and flipped to the verse. "'Consider it pure joy, my brothers and sisters, whenever you face trials of many kinds because you know that the testing of your faith produces perseverance. Let perseverance finish its work so that you may be mature and complete, not lacking anything.'[7] In other words, the final chapter of the journey will be joyous."

Bill looked up at me. "King Solomon wrote that when storms sweep by, the righteous will be found to have stood firm.[8] I think he's saying that life is like a grindstone. Whether it wears you down or polishes you up depends upon what you are made of."

I smiled. "My grandfather used to tell me and my brothers, 'When you're squeezed, what's inside will gush out.'"

"That's why it's good to have God's Spirit and his word in your heart." Bill finished his orange juice. "I need to get to some cows that need tending to. But I think you're learning some valuable lessons, young man. We should live in a present that is defined by our future, not our past. Live life rooted in your will-be's instead of wallowing in your were's or was'es. What will be is ultimately and eternally more important than what has been or what is."

"Which means?"

Bill opened his Bible again and turned the pages. "Here it is. Peter wrote, 'Be glad for the chance to suffer as Christ suffered. It will prepare you for even greater happiness when he makes his glorious return.'"[9] He shut the Bible. "Paul wrote that any sorrows, storms, or suffering we go through in this life could not even begin to compare with the glory and joy that will be shown to us in the future.[10] Make sense?"

"I think so, Bill."

"Until next week?"

"You bet," I responded before he headed out. As always, my mentor left me with a lot more than breakfast to digest.

7

Imminent Calamity

PASTOR PETE ZIEG AND HIS WIFE, Judy, were expecting their first grandchild courtesy of their oldest son, Mark, and his wife, Laura. Due to a uterine anomaly discovered in a prenatal ultrasound, Dr. Pratt felt the safest way to deliver the baby was a Cesarean. We scheduled the surgery for the Wednesday after Thanksgiving.

That crisp autumn day was gray, overcast, and surprisingly foggy, but the mood inside the labor and delivery suite was one of happy expectation. Dr. Pratt, Sandi Lynch, a labor and delivery nurse, and I scrubbed as the anesthesiologist administered Laura's spinal block anesthesia for complete loss of feeling below her waist. After prepping and draping her, the surgery went as expected. We delivered a healthy-looking baby boy. I quickly showed him to Mark and Laura. Until then, they had not wanted to know the gender. "Does he have a name?" I asked.

Laura smiled and said, "Jonathan."

"Well come, Jonathan." I turned and took him to the warmer and waiting nurses, who stimulated him with warm towels. Then the unexpected struck. Jonathan's eyes widened, but he was not breathing.

"Suction," I said. One nurse handed a tiny suction catheter to me, and I suctioned his nose, mouth, and pharynx. The nurses hooked up a cardiac monitor and taped a pulse oximeter to one of his big toes. The oximeter was a recent technology for measuring the oxygen concentration transcutaneously.

"Heart rate 40, pulse ox 70," one nurse said. Both were critically low. Jonathan still was not breathing and was turning bluer by the second. My heart was racing as I took his feet in one hand and used the middle three fingers of my other hand to "spank" the soles of his feet to surprise him and get him to breathe. He didn't respond. The baby boy was turning a dark purple from lack of oxygen.

"Let's begin CPR!" I said, trying to sound much calmer than I felt. Inside I was terrified.

One nurse began gentle chest compressions using the tips of two fingers in the center of Jonathan's chest as she hummed the Bee Gee's pop hit, "Stayin' Alive," which had the perfect tempo of 100 to 120 beats per minute. It was an old trick that helped keep the proper rate.

"Ambu bag, please!" I said. A nurse handed me a small bag that was connected to oxygen. It was a handheld device used to provide positive pressure ventilation to patients who were not breathing or not breathing adequately. I attached a small mask, opened the airway by lifting the baby's chin, covered his mouth and nose with the mask, and squeezed the bag to give two breaths, each about one second long. I expected to see the baby's chest rise with each breath, but it looked uneven. *What's that mean?* I thought as I felt my heartbeat quicken.

"Pause!" The pulse and oxygen levels continued to drop precipitously. "Restart!" I commanded as I administered two more breaths. Once again, the chest didn't rise as I expected. Something was blocking the oxygen from getting to the lungs. I began to panic. This precious baby was dying right in front of my eyes. What happened in the next few moments would mean life or death.

I turned and grabbed a laryngoscope handle and snapped on a tongue blade. I checked the battery by making sure the light at the end worked. This instrument would help me intubate Jonathan—a procedure in which I'd put a tube down his throat and into his windpipe, making it easier to get air into and out of his lungs.

The laryngoscope was designed to help me look past the baby's tongue and down the throat. If something was blocking the trachea that I could not easily remove, that meant emergency tracheostomy. I was scared to death of the possibility because that was a procedure I'd never done on a newborn. Hopefully Allan or the anesthesiologist could help me.

One nurse dabbed the sweat pouring down my forehead. After double-checking that Jonathan's body was aligned straight, I gently extended his head with my right hand. I pushed down on the baby's larynx with the fifth finger of my left hand, the laryngoscope in my left hand. This gentle pressure would position the vocal cords for visualization.

"I can see the cords!" I exclaimed. It felt like a ton of bricks rolled off my shoulders.

With my right hand, I picked up a small endotracheal tube and gently guided it down and between the vocal cords so the tip of the tube was about one centimeter below the vocal cords.

"Ambu bag," I said.

The nurse attached it to the tube as I held the tube firmly in place.

"Bag him!" I ordered. The right chest immediately filled with each breath, but not the left. Fortunately the baby's oxygen levels rapidly normalized as the nurse continued to bag him.

"Pause," I said to the nurse doing compressions. My stress level plummeted as he began to pink up, grimace, and move all four extremities to stimulation. "Praise the Lord!" I whispered as I re-examined him.

I secured the endotracheal tube with tape, then grabbed a neonatal stethoscope and listened to the chest. Breath sounds were loud and clear in the right lung, but there was minimal airflow on the left. I heard strange sounds but wasn't sure what they were. Then, to my horror, I realized what I heard: bowel sounds!

"Call radiology. We need a stat chest X-ray," I told a nurse. "Also, call a respiratory therapist to bring a Baby Bear." This was a mechanical ventilator for newborns. As she left, I looked at the other nurse. "Set up for a stat umbilical artery catheterization." I needed to pass a tiny catheter into and down one of the umbilical arteries in the umbilical cord's stump for administering medications and drawing blood samples.

Allan and Sandi walked up beside me. "Laura's stable. She and Mark are in the recovery room," Allan said. I hadn't even noticed the nurses taking Laura out of the OR.

"What's the problem with the little guy?" Allan asked.

"I'm not 100 percent sure. Listen." I handed him the stethoscope and held the bell over the left chest.

"Diaphragmatic hernia?" Allan's eyes widened.

I nodded. He referred to a rare defect in which there is an abnormal opening in the baby's diaphragm, the muscle between the lungs and the stomach that enables proper breathing. But the hernia allows the baby's intestines to move from the belly into the chest cavity. It occurs while the baby is developing in the womb and usually only involves one side—most commonly the left. Either way, the lung tissue and blood vessels on the affected side may not develop.

"Want me to call Arnold Palmer?" Sandi asked, referring to the regional children's hospital in Orlando.

I nodded.

"Life Flight?" she asked.

"It would be best. The sooner this baby is in the neonatal ICU, the better."

The team all nodded. "Want me to let Mark and Laura know what's going on?" Allan asked.

"That would be great. Tell them I'll be there as soon as possible."

Allan and Sandi left as a technician rolled the X-ray machine in and took the needed pictures. "Back in a moment with the film," the technician said.

I turned to the nurses. "We'll do the umbilical catheter and set up the ventilator in the nursery. We'll also need to place a vented orogastric tube." That was a thin tube passed down the mouth and esophagus into the stomach. It would be connected to continuous low suction to remove any gas that formed in the stomach to prevent bowel distension and further lung compression. "We want as little gas in the stomach as possible," I said. "And I'll need to talk to the intake doctor at the NICU. Ready to transport?"

They nodded as Hamp Sessions, MD, a radiologist at the hospital, rushed into the room with the film. He popped it into the X-ray viewer and turned it on. "Just what you suspected, Walt. Bowel contents in the entire left chest, the tip of the endotracheal tube is in perfect position, and the right lung and heart appear normal."

"Thank the Lord, the baby's vital signs are now normal," I added.

"He's sure a beautiful pink, isn't he?" Hamp said.

"Now, but not when we started!"

"I suspect not."

"Everything looked healthy on the prenatal ultrasound I did. How did I miss this?" I asked.

"In which trimester did you do it?"

"It was an early second-trimester ultrasound. About thirteen weeks."

"You probably did *not* miss it. It's difficult to diagnose before twenty-four weeks gestation, and 10 to 20 percent of the time, it's not even seen later in pregnancy."

"Well, that makes me feel better. Thanks, Hamp."

"Ready to roll?" one nurse said.

"Let's go!"

In the nursery, I placed the umbilical catheter and orogastric tubes. After starting IV fluids, the initial labs and vital signs were all normal—at least for the moment.

We were ready for Life Flight and the helicopter couldn't get here soon enough.[1]

8

Baptism under Fire

THE ARNOLD PALMER HOSPITAL for Children and Women in downtown Orlando—a distance of twenty miles as the crow flies—had agreed to the emergency air transfer. They also had reviewed and approved my treatment plan. Unfortunately, the weather had deteriorated and would not allow a helicopter transport, so they decided to send their specialized infant rescue vehicle. It would take an hour or more for them to arrive.

Jonathan took a turn for the worse. His respiratory and heart rates increased, as did his respiratory effort. Then his oxygen level dropped. Hamp brought the film from the stat chest X-ray I ordered and flipped it up on the view box.

"Right-sided pneumothorax, Walt. I'd estimate 25 to 35 percent. Maybe more." This meant that the lung must have developed a small tear and was leaking air into the chest cavity but outside the lung. Since the free air had no way to escape, it built up pressure and compressed the remaining lung, resulting in Jonathan's increasing distress.

"Endotracheal tube's still in a good position," Hamp continued, "as are the orogastric tube and the umbilical catheter. The bowel in the left chest has no more gas, which is good. That tells me the orogastric suction is doing the job. But it looks like this guy's going to need a stat chest tube."

"No doubt," I replied. Turning to Sandi, I said, "Let's set it up!"

With no functioning left lung and right lung volume reduced, Jonathan was operating on only about one-third of a normal baby's respiratory capacity. Worse, if the pneumothorax grew, it would squeeze Jonathan's one remaining lung and could quickly kill him. He needed a chest tube, a small plastic tube, inserted between two ribs into the lung's pleural space. When the tube is connected to a suction machine, the leaking air is drained from the chest cavity, allowing the lung to work correctly.

But the transport team, which could easily do this procedure, was nowhere near, and I had not done a pediatric chest tube in years. In fact, I could only remember having done one or two in my training.

Fortunately, I had done quite a few on adults successfully, and the procedure is almost identical. The circumstances were not ideal, but given Jonathan's rapidly deteriorating condition, I had no choice. It would be another life-or-death moment for this little guy.

"Could have happened from excess pressure during the resuscitation or with the ventilator," Hamp commented as he examined the film. "Or he may have just had a congenital weakness in the lining of the lung that ruptured, like a bleb or blister. No way to know from the X-ray."

I thought back on the multiple pneumothoraxes, or collapsed lungs, I had personally experienced in college and medical school. Mine were caused when congenital blebs on my left lung would spontaneously leak air into my chest cavity once or twice a year. They were quite painful, but all of mine were much smaller than this one and resolved without a chest tube. Nevertheless, during my internship, because mine were happening more frequently and getting larger each time, one of the chest surgeons had to go in

and remove the blebs to prevent any more or any worse pneumothoraxes. The surgery was a success.

In Jonathan's case, if the procedure was unsuccessful and his
pneumothorax expanded, he'd have no way to get enough oxygen
into his bloodstream. He would die. I had no pediatric surgeon at
our hospital to call. My anxiety levels were rising by the minute.
I thought through the procedure. I would have to prep and numb
the skin over his lower chest wall, use a scalpel to make a small
hole in the chest cavity, insert a small tube into it, and connect
that to suction. This would hopefully pull the unwanted air out
and expand the lung.

To save Jonathan's life, I had to risk performing the procedure.
I could only pray a psalm that popped into my head, *"You are my
helper and my deliverer; my God, do not delay!"*[1]

I prayed silently during the entire stat procedure. Thankfully
it was an instant success. Jonathan's vital signs and oxygen level
quickly normalized. I ordered a stat X-ray, and Hamp ran back
into the nursery with the post-procedure film, saying, "Success!"
We both could see that the pneumothorax was gone. *Thank you,
Lord!* I silently prayed, yet again.

At that moment, the transport team from Arnold Palmer rushed
in. It was great to have them there finally! The medical personnel quickly reviewed everything we had done, swarmed over and
around Jonathan, checking every detail. They changed our con-
nections to those in the transport incubator and placed him in it.
He remained stable during the entire process.

The head of the team, Kelly, who was also a NICU advanced
nurse practitioner, said, "Good job, Dr. Larimore. I think we're
ready to roll."

"What do you think caused the pneumothorax?" I asked.

"Mechanical ventilation or CPR can cause it," she replied.
"We see it all the time in the NICU because it's common in newborns who have underlying lung disease. But no matter the cause,
neonatal pneumothorax is a life-threatening condition, and it's

associated with a high incidence of morbidity and mortality. You handled it perfectly and likely saved this little guy's life. Well done. Would you mind if I went with you to talk to Mom and Dad?"

Just at that moment, Sandi, our nurse, walked in. "Mark's parents, Pastor Pete and Judy, are with him and Laura. They are all more or less stunned and numb. I'm assuming you will want to talk to them all."

"Of course! Sandi, let's roll this little one out to his parents and introduce them. It will only be for a few moments."

"My team can take a short coffee break while I join you," Kelly said.

When we entered Laura's room, the tension, apprehension, and worry were unmistakable. Laura, Mark, Pete, and Judy all looked to be in a state of shock. But once they saw Jonathan, with his eyes wide open, despite all of the tubes and the ventilator, the relief was palpable. I introduced Kelly to the Ziegs and we moved the incubator by the bed, so Laura was able to roll toward her baby, put her hand through a portal, and gently stroke and hold his tiny foot. I explained the hernia, the CPR process, the pneumothorax, all the tubes, and his current condition.

As tears streaked down her face, Laura noted, "But he looks so normal."

"As far as I can tell, other than the hernia, he is," Kelly said. "Have you named him?"

"Jonathan Andrew," Laura said.

"Let me give you all some idea of what will happen next." She explained the transfer process, the NICU care, and the likely surgery. "About half of all newborns who have diaphragmatic hernia will also have other conditions, including other congenital abnormalities, but the team at the children's hospital will test that thoroughly."

"What causes the hernia?" Mark asked.

"It's usually unknown," Kelly explained. "But if we find the cause, we'll sure tell you."

"How long is the recovery?" Pastor Pete asked.

"I can't predict that right now," she said. "The important thing is he's cleared his first hurdles with flying colors and is in great shape at the moment."

Pastor Pete's face tightened. "He's our first grandchild. What is the chance he might not survive this severe, invisible deformity? I mean, otherwise, he does look perfect."

"The mortality rates for congenital diaphragmatic hernia have remained at about 30 percent over the last couple of decades. Given the fact Dr. Larimore resuscitated him so quickly, and with him looking so fit, I have great hope that he'll beat those odds. Especially with the newer treatments we have these days."

"Newer treatments?" Pete asked.

"Jonathan will need enough oxygen in his system while they give him some time for his lungs to recover from the shock of all this. We're using a newer technique called ECMO or extracorporeal membrane oxygenation. It uses a tiny pump to circulate his blood through an artificial lung and then back into the bloodstream. It can be lifesaving in cases like this. But the next few days and weeks will be critical."

"We need a miracle, Dr. Walt," Pete whispered, as his eyes filled with tears. Judy reached up to take his hand.

"You've already had several, but one especially big one," Kelly said softly. "A normal vaginal delivery would have dramatically decreased his chances for survival. So, in this instance, the Cesarean was a gift. Thank God for *that* miracle! But we need to get him on the road."

"Do we have a moment for a quick prayer—to ask for more miracles?" I asked.

Kelly nodded, and I said a prayer of thanks for Jonathan, asked for the Lord's healing touch to be upon him, for safety in the transport, and for wisdom for the team that would care for him. After I said, "Amen," Pete turned to Mark and Laura. "Would it be okay if I baptize him?"

Mark looked at Laura, who nodded and then turned to us. "Dad, that would be wonderful."

Smiling, Kelly said, "Of course! But it needs to be quick."

I glanced at Sandi, who beamed and nodded. "Pastor, may I get you a little sterile water?"

"That would be perfect," Pete said.

While we waited for Sandi to return, Pete explained, "Emergency baptism of infants in this kind of circumstance is not an unusual practice for not only us Lutherans but also several other denominations, including Methodists, Episcopalians, Catholics, and Presbyterians. We believe it brings the assurance that the one baptized is a child of God, joined to Christ now and forever, no matter what happens."

I knew the moment was sacred, but I couldn't help offering a small joke: "Even though Jonathan's intubated, I'd suggest we not do baptism by immersion."

Everyone chuckled. Pastor Pete washed his hands and said, "Walt, as you know, I'm Lutheran, *not* a Baptist."

Sandi returned with a small container of sterile water. Jonathan was wide awake, seeming to take note of the whole event as Grandpa Pete performed the ceremony by inserting his hand into the incubator, sprinkling a few drops of water on Jonathan's tiny head three times, and said, "Jonathan Andrew Zieg, I baptize you in the name of the Father, and of the Son, and of the Holy Spirit. Amen."

Pete then traced the sign of the cross upon his tiny forehead and said, "Jonathan, child of God, you have been sealed by the Holy Spirit and marked with the cross of Christ forever. You are already a miracle to us, and we ask our Father in heaven to give you more miracles down the road."

It was one of the holiest moments of my medical career. The transport team left, and within the hour, Jonathan was in the NICU at Arnold Palmer. Once he was connected to ECMO, he quickly stabilized but had to stay on the ventilator. Then he was approved for the first of what would be a series of surgeries to correct the deformity. His estimated chance of survival was around 70 percent and even though it was several weeks before the family could hold him, he continued to improve. One important reason, as one of Jonathan's ICU specialists told Pastor Pete later, was that "those who are prayed for seem to do better." He was correct.

It was a long and winding road, with more than a few setbacks, but the Lord graciously answered all of our prayers. Years later, Pastor Pete sent this email update:

> Thanks be to God! Jonathan could have died or been brain damaged because of a lack of oxygen. He recovered and grew up with minimal difficulty. He is now a brilliant, articulate twenty-five-year-old, who is nearly six feet tall and recently graduated from college with a Bachelor of Science degree and dual majors in chemistry and computer science.[2]

I stared at my screen and whispered a silent prayer of thanks. But I also felt humbled that God allowed me to be part of this miracle.

The miracle of life.

9

Rodeo Time

IT WAS TIME FOR THE SILVER SPURS RODEO, which occurs in Kissimmee twice a year. It's one of the fifty largest in the country, the largest east of the Mississippi River, and Florida's official state rodeo. After I moved to town, the Spurs' doctor, Hamp Sessions, passed the reins on to me.

"My dad's best friend is Geech Partin," he told me one time in the concession stand, where he was flipping burgers. "They hunted and just hung around. Our families did a lot together, as Geech and Connie had five children, as did my parents. We were all about the same ages. All of our Thanksgivings were spent at the Partins' Fanny Bass Pasture Camp on Lake Toho. I don't think Geech ever owned a watch, so if you were to meet him somewhere in the woods, you just counted on a little latitude for the time. He was such an optimist and so much fun to be around.

"We loved to get Geech to sing the old cowboy ballad, 'The Sierry Peaks,' though I'm not sure of the exact name. It was about two drunk cattle-rustling cowboys confronted by the devil who wanted to gather their souls and take them to hell. Given the devil had horns and a tail, the cowboys just lassoed him, branded him, pruned his horns with a dehorning saw, and knotted his tail for a joke."

Hamp laughed. "Geech loved singing that old song. And he loved teaching me, my older brother, and his boys so much about hunting. My favorite admonition of his was, 'If you kill it, you've got to eat it—other than rattlesnakes and cottonmouths!'"

"I've enjoyed my time with Geech and Connie," I said, "and I consider it an honor to be able to help out the Spurs."

Hamp set down his spatula. "As a radiologist, I've never been entirely comfortable as the rodeo doc, but given what Geech tells me about you and what I've seen of your doctoring, I suspect the role will fit you like a glove. Besides, I'd rather be in the concession stand flipping burgers. Somehow, I really enjoy that. Takes my mind off of my practice and my worries!"

John joined me for the Friday competition, the first of three days of events. I had parked my old truck in a reserved space by the grandstand that was filled with a sold-out, standing-room-only audience of eight thousand. Then John and I checked in with Alice Ramsey, who ran the First-Aid room. From there, we went up the steps to the announcer's booth, greeting friends along the way, including Kathy Baker, the Spurs' secretary, and their favorite announcer, Clem McSpadden, who came all the way from Oklahoma. I liked visiting Clem in his announcer's booth before each rodeo, as he was a walking encyclopedia of rodeo trivia and tales.

After our visit, and before the competition, I returned to the concession stand to visit with our office receptionist, Jean Parten, who was working alongside Geech's wife, Connie, who had been supervising this particular concession stand for decades. Hamp was still at the grill cooking mouthwatering burgers with a big smile, clearly in his element.

"What'll it be?" Jean asked us. "Everything's on the house for you guys."

John and I placed and carted our takeout orders to the sitting area outside the First-Aid room, next to the arena. As the events began, we enjoyed the aromas and mouthwatering tastes of our freshly grilled Angus-beef burgers, slathered with a secret-recipe sauce Connie had developed, with a side of hand-cut curly fries and ice-cold Coca-Colas. When mixed with the powerful whiffs from the stock, the bucolic perfume arising from the moist arena soil, and the delectable scents of cotton candy and popcorn that wafted across the stadium, this seemed like a slice of Americana.

A high-pitched whine grabbed my attention. I turned to see Geech Partin approaching on a battery-powered scooter, which made sense. As his physician, I knew he now had severe arthritis in his neck, back, hips, and knees, gained from many years of rodeoing, ranching, and having fallen off a "few too many rank stock," as he would say. If there was ever a candidate for joint replacement surgery, Geech Partin was it.

"Have you rodeoed a lot?" John asked Geech. He didn't know as much about Geech's past as I did.

"My whole life," Geech replied. "Knew how to ride a horse before I could pedal a bike. But to really rodeo, you gotta be a cowboy. Our hard work on the range brings us together—gives us a bond. It defines us on the ranch and in the arena. When you walk away from most rodeos, you've not only not made any money but you've actually lost it."

"So why did you rodeo?" John asked.

"I just wanted to gain some respect from my friends and the gals." He winked. "Winning a gold or silver belt buckle was the icing on the cake. Who don't want that? It lit a fire in me to ride the best I could. Sure, I wanted some prize money, but it was striving to make that perfect ride and that feeling you get when you best a bull that's not only trying to get you off his back as hard as he can but hurt you in the process. Adrenaline and heart-squeezing fear wrapped on top of a ton of fury. But you got to learn how to control it. Otherwise, things go downhill pretty quick."

"Did your rodeo injuries put you on this new buggy of yours?" John asked, smiling.

"The sport takes a toll on your body and your family. Eventually, the injuries catch up with you, and you're forced to spend more time on the ranch and less time in the arena. There are no big NFL salaries in rodeo, but there are common injuries that would make a football running back or linebacker cringe. While the bulls and horses are rarely injured, that's not true for the riders. These days, they all have their family doctor on speed dial."

"I bet you did," I interjected.

"Yeah. I had to. Over the years, I had a fractured skull, a broken back, busted knees, a broken nose about ten times, plus broken sinus bones and fingers. Oh, and there was a brain bleed one time. But all of them hurt a lot less than the heartbreak of being thrown off. In rodeo we say, 'When the storm is raging, just hold on!'"

"Sounds a lot like life," I said. "We all get thrown around from time to time."

"This is what I tell the kids," Geech said. "God does not give us an overcoming life, he gives us life to overcome. And he gives life as we overcome. The rough rides can give the strength. If there ain't no trials, there ain't no strength. When you face the tornado, he'll give you the strength to survive the thing. But he don't necessarily give you strength when you don't need it."

Just then, the rodeo band struck up a fast country tune. We had a perfect view across the arena from our place by the First-Aid stand. Suddenly, the first bull was released with a cowboy hanging on for dear life. "The Spurs always start and end the rodeo with bull riding. The fans love it," I informed John.

Before I could finish the statement, the rider was tossed to the ground. As the bull turned to thunder after him, the fallen cowboy picked himself up and raced to the steel fence. In a flash, the two bullfighters, in full clown regalia, ran between the beast and the thrown rider. One of them ran and swatted its nose as he passed. The bull had turned to chase him when the other bullfighter attempted the same. This time the bull lowered and swung his head. One of his horns caught the bullfighter in the middle of his chest and flung him to the ground. The crowd gasped and hushed. He lay like a ragdoll, not moving a muscle.

The upright bullfighter distracted the bull as the three pick-up men on their Quarter Horses raced toward the beast. One pick-up cowboy lassoed the bull and hauled it toward a gate leading out of the arena.

The uninjured bullfighter gingerly helped his buddy to his feet and walked him in our direction. He was hunched over and clearly in pain. We let him in through a steel gate and took him inside. I quickly examined the bullfighter and determined his abdomen, heart, and lungs were normal. But his chest wall was not doing so well.

He grimaced as I palpated his sternum and ribs. I probed with my fingers, causing him more pain. When I was finished, I announced, "You have at least four broken ribs."

"That's all?!" he exclaimed. "I was hoping for a new record. I've had five before."

I smiled. Rodeo competitors and bullfighters were some of the toughest folks I ever treated. Their pain thresholds were sky-high but so was the goodness of their hearts and characters.

"If you could inject a little lidocaine around each fracture and tape me up real good, I should be good to go. My buddies need me out there."

"I can do better than that," I told him. "I have a longer-lasting anesthetic. It's called *Marcaine*. It'll last several hours, but you still won't be as agile, partner."

"He will be, Doc," Geech observed. "You can bet on it."

When I finished taping him up and sent him on his way, I marveled how cowboys were able to overlook their pain and focus on the goal of doing their job—in this case, of being a bullfighter. He knew that most of his actions on the arena floor—overlooked by many in the audience—could save a fallen rider from injuries far more severe than four broken ribs.

I now saw why calling the bullfighters clowns was a mistake. I could see why some might call them crazy, but after today, I would call them heroes. I think most cowboys would.

Geech was both a patient and a dear friend, and he served as my tour guide to all things cowboy and rodeo. There wasn't a Silver Spurs event at which I didn't learn something from this walking encyclopedia of equestrian, equine, bovine, and stockman information and history—as well as some of the commonsense practical sides of real life.

"Rodeo is America's original pastime," he said while John and I joined him on the side of the arena the next day. "Along with wrestling and hockey, it's one of the last blue-collar sports in America. It started in the Old West with an event called *saddle bronc*. It's one of our last reminders of the American frontier.

"The stock and the riders are randomly paired together during each rodeo. Both have to perform well to get a good score from the judges. When it comes to bull riding, they always put the rankest bulls and best riders in the rodeo's last session. It's what everyone comes for, and until the last rider, no one will leave."

As we pulled up our chairs outside the First-Aid room and behind the protective steel fencing, Geech gave us a running commentary. "They'll be starting the last bull rides here in a minute. Just you wait and see," he said.

John had a question. "Do all the bucking events have the same rules as far as having to ride for eight seconds?"

"Yep. You not only gotta hold on eight seconds, but you have to hold on with style to an animal especially bred to buck ya off. You're kinda dancing with the animal. Most of us tend to dance better with a mean ole bull than we do our gals. Bull riding is a collaborative sport. One fella said it was like a pairs competition where one partner tries to kill the other, like an ice dance with an ax murderer."[1] Geech laughed out loud at his description.

"To receive a good score, the rider's gotta draw a rank bull," he told us. "The meaner the animal, the better the tally. The rider not only has to stay on the full eight seconds, but his free hand can't touch the bull or his own self anywhere. One touch will cause a judge to throw the red flag for a disqualification—what we call a DQ. And it don't mean Dairy Queen." Geech chuckled.

"Surely there are easier ways to make a living?" John observed.

Geech thought this through for a moment. "Easier, I think so. But better? I don't know. Probably not."

"Even with all the injuries and the way it's got you crippled a bit now?" John asked.

Geech turned reflective for a moment, then commented, "Mama used to tell me over and over, 'Remember. The good Lord loves you. The good Lord watches over you—no matter where you go or what you do.' I went through quite a few days wandering from the straight and narrow, and cowboying hobbled me up a bit. But I wouldn't go back and change a thing. I've learned pain in life is guaranteed, but suffering is up to us. And Mama's words, the good Lord's love, and my wonderful wife and kids have brought me to a better place—a more peaceful pasture. That's what gets me through these days. That's what comforts my soul when my body's not so well. Now, I'm in about as good a place as I could be."

He sat back in his scooter. "Doc, I ain't sure how much time I've got. But I'm gonna enjoy every minute of what's left. And I'm glad I've got you doctors to help me cross that river when it's time."

I thought I saw his eyes mist as he was quiet for a moment. *He's on another range in another time*, I thought.

A smile of deep satisfaction spread across his face, deepening my faith that this wouldn't be our last rodeo together.[2]

10

Don't Lose the Lesson

LATER THAT DAY WE WATCHED the cowboys preparing their ropes in the chutes from the safety of the First-Aid station. All the riders wore vests, and some wore helmets, which was a relatively new development. John noticed too, and asked Geech about it.

"American bull riding is called 'the most dangerous eight seconds in sports.' I think it's true. Bareback has more injuries, but bull riding has more deaths. Most of the men wear a protective vest. So do the rodeo clowns, bullfighters, and most bronc riders. The vest offers some powerful protection from direct trauma, such as getting stomped on or sliced with a horn, saving many a cowboy's life. You'll see." Geech nodded toward the arena. "But the helmets are newer. They've only been around a few years. Supposed to prevent a man from having his skull or face split open, broken, or crushed. Some folks want 'em required, but I don't think that's ever gonna happen. Cowboys like independence. Other people believe the weight of the helmet may increase neck injuries. Time'll tell."

"Guess they're some pretty tough men," John said.

"Believe it or not, most of 'em are religious—or at least they become that way," Geech said, chuckling. "The old-timers say, 'Riding bulls is a Jesus trap.' Bullriders don't pray because they want to, they pray because they have to. They know they need some extra protection from above."

Geech took a breath. "And maybe they're a bit crazy too. I always say, 'If lawyers are disbarred, and clergymen are defrocked, shouldn't it follow that cowboys are deranged?'"

John and I laughed. I admired Geech's unfathomably deep pool of homespun humor.

"But even the craziest cowboy is not as unhinged as those dern bulls," he continued. "Rodeo bulls are unreasonable, unpredictable, and irrational creatures. They can be skittish one moment and downright crazy and cantankerous the next. They're as likely to lie down in the chute as they are to gore you. Over the decades, selective breeding has made rodeo bulls more dangerous and, as a result, more valuable than ever before. The best ones cost over a hundred thousand dollars, and their semen can fetch thousands."

"Do they go through any special training?" John asked.

Geech chuckled at the question and looked at me. "Why, your partner's almost as naive about this as you used to be, Doc."

"Well, we both know a lot more about human medicine than we do animals, that's for sure," I said.

Geech turned back to John. "I've found most animals don't like to have anything on their backs. Most try to shake off whatever's there. More often than not, stock knuckle under and are broken when all is said and done. That ain't the case for rodeo bulls. They ain't built for submission, and not only will they toss riders for the pure joy of it but they will invent even more impressive ways to smack 'em off. They actually learn as they gain more experience."

"They're that smart?" John asked.

"You bet your hide. A young bull may sprint around the ring, throwing in jumps and an occasional spin. As he gets older, he not only gets less predictable, but he can get downright nasty. He'll spin one way and then the other. Never the same way twice. He may charge forward, then jerk to one side, then whirl. The great ones look like they're hinged in the middle. Their front end jerks one way while the back end jackhammers the other. In between, his spine'll twist and gyrate so the rider has no balancing point. His center of gravity changes from second to second. He's stronger than any cowboy's clenched fist, all hoof and horn with nothing but nasty, fast-twitch muscle in between."

"I see why cowboys wear that protective gear."

"Don't always help. Last year I was down south of here at the Okeechobee Cowtown Rodeo. There was a National Champion bull mounted by a rookie cowboy. Had his vest and a helmet with a face guard. Right outta the chute, that nasty bull bucked with all his might and dropped his front shoulders real low.

"The rider leaned back and threw his free arm back for balance, but that bull sensed the move and reacted in a bucking motion that threw the cowboy forward toward his head. As the rider was thrown forward, that beast thrust his head up and smashed it smack dab into that cowboy's face—helmet, face guard, and all.

"The boy was knocked out cold and should have been tossed, but his hand got twisted up in the rope while that bull spun like a top. Would've ripped his arm off if the bullfighters hadn't jumped in. May have saved his life, but not his face or arm." Geech shook his head. "That boy's rotator cuff was torn to pieces, and every bone in his face was broken. He spent several hours in surgery that day and had at least a dozen reconstructive surgeries after that. They say he never regained taste or smell, and he'll never ride again."

John grimaced. "Guess I can see why y'all want docs like Walt and me here for each rodeo."

"And the paramedics. It don't go wrong often, but when it does, it can get real ugly real fast."

"With the risk, the injuries, the pain, why do they keep doing it year after year?"

Geech pushed his hat back and scratched his head, pondering.

"There're different reasons for each man. They *all* know it's dangerous. It ain't if'n a man's gonna get hurt, it's when. But the bottom line is, for most, there's more glory in it than injuries. Most of the pain goes away—although some've gotta wait longer than others. They're accustomed to keeping their pain to themselves. That's one reason most of 'em won't come here to the First-Aid stand to see you. Gotta pretty much drag 'em here."

"That I've figured out," John commented.

I spoke up. "I get it that none of them are doing it for the money. But it seems like, if you compare the hazards to the possible rewards, it's a pretty dangerous sport. It's hard to believe that these fellows risk their lives and limbs like this."

"Doc, you gotta understand that it all goes back to the first time they got on a sheep as a kiddo, a calf as a boy, or a bull as a young man. They got thrown off or bucked off, hit that ground hard, and got their breath knocked clear out or their bell rung. But they jumped up to the cheer of the crowd and the backslapping from the other cowboys. Right then and there, they knew that this was what they was built to do. I think most of 'em believe it's better to be a has-been than a never-was.

"And," Geech continued, "it teaches 'bout life. What they learn in rodeoing is that when the draw gives you a lousy bronc or bull to ride, you can run from it, you can sit back and let it toss you around however it wants, or you can suit up, buckle up, grip that son-of-a-gun, and man up, give it your best, and see what the good Lord has in store for you. The goal is to do the best you can, to do what you're meant to do, with people you love and who love you.

"Sometimes you're a winner, with all the honor and glory—not to mention the belt buckle, prize money, and saddle that go with it. But more often than not, you finish your ride, dust yourself off, tend to your scrapes and bruises, and know you done your best." Geech had a far-off look in his eye. "In the end, a cowboy learns you don't let troubles or trials bring the fight to you. Instead, you must take the fight to the storm. Cowboys pride themselves on never backing down on what they're called to do, no matter the obstacles or odds. Like I tell my boys, 'When you lose, don't lose the lesson.'"

I felt like I was having breakfast in Joanie's Diner with a different mentor—but the teaching was just as applicable. I prayed I had the ears to hear what Geech was teaching and was grateful for the opportunity to learn.

Geech shared Bill Judge's wisdom—only from another lens of experience and expressed in another unique language. While Bill's was scriptural, Geech's was salt of the earth. Both were universal.

"Hey, Doc!" I turned to see the injured bullfighter walking toward me. He was grimacing but upright and still moving with purpose. "Mind giving these fractures another dose of that Marcaine?"

I nodded. "Absolutely not. Come on in."

"They don't make 'em tougher or better," Geech whispered, his respect and admiration evident.

They certainly don't.

The next time I stubbed my toe walking to the bathroom in the middle of the night and hobbled back to my bed complaining, I resolved to remember what those cowboys dealt with every day and the vast admiration I was developing for them.[1]

11

Quality Time

My family's time in our rental home was not uneventful, so I was more committed than ever to have our family sit together for breakfast and supper as often as possible. Barb and I believed that quality time as a family only occurs within quantity time. When we spent time as a family, sharing not only the details of our day but also our opinions, emotions, and hearts, we enjoyed our time together and also grew closer.

One night at dinner, when Scott was complaining about his troubles with the way a particular teacher was teaching a subject in which he was doing very poorly, Kate made an observation. "Scott, I have cerebral palsy and only half a brain, and I made a B in that class."

Scott blushed and looked at me as if to express, *What's the comeback to that?*

I smiled, shrugged, and thought of Geech. "As Mr. Partin would say, 'You got got real good!'"

Making our mealtimes a priority wasn't always easy to accomplish. We found pleasant family mealtimes don't just happen by accident but are the result of deliberate decisions and actions. For example, we refused to answer phone calls during meals. We used an answering machine during all mealtimes. For us, these times together became sacred—a time when we could each share deeply about anything. It was also a time for Barb and me to share our joys, concerns, and values with the kids and each other. Therefore, when one of the kids would answer the phone while we were preparing for dinner, I'd say, "Tell them I'm not here."

One night at dinner, Scott asked, "Dad, why do you make me tell a lie? Doesn't the Lord hate a lying tongue?"[1]

Ouch! Busted! My aim in guarding our family time was commendable, but I was asking my children to lie and that was just plain wrong. We talked about the issue that night at the table, and I admitted that I had been wrong and thanked Scott for pointing it out to me. It was an important lesson for me about what was required to turn values into virtues. I asked Scott, in the future, to say that I was unavailable at the moment but that he would be happy to take a message.

Another evening, while sharing events of the day, Kate said, "I got bullied today at school, but Tina took care of it." Because of her noticeable limp from her difficulty using her body's left side and a slight speech impediment, classmates constantly bullied Kate. *Handicap*, *retard*, *spastic*, and *limper* were just a few of the verbal jabs she learned to ignore.

When we arrived in Kissimmee, second-grader Kate met her best friend, Tina Rinkus. Little Tina was not the ignoring kind and confronted Kate's verbal bullies nose-to-nose. Her father, Don Rinkus, taught driver's education at Osceola High School, so no one but no one could get their driver's license without his approval. Knowing that, most of these persecutors would back down.

"What happened?" I asked Kate that evening.

"We were sitting by ourselves at lunch. Three older boys came to sit across from us and began making fun of me. I ignored them, but Tina did not. She asked them to stop and leave, or else. One of them made the mistake of saying something like, 'Or what else, pipsqueak? I've got a mind to slap you silly, you moron. Why do you sit with this retard anyway? Are you ignorant—or just another nobody?'"

"Oh my," Barb said. "Then what?"

"Tina's face turned red," Kate said, "and then she stood up and left! It scared me. I couldn't imagine why she had abandoned me. I mean, she's my very best friend *ever*. The boys kept mocking me, but I tried to ignore them. Some people say sticks and stones may break your bones, but words can never hurt you, but that's not true. Words can hurt. They hurt me." Kate took a deep breath. "Then it happened."

"What?" Barb asked.

"Six big football players came up behind them. Two of the players picked up each boy and carried him out through the cafeteria door. Tina sat down beside me and said, 'Well, that takes care of that. We don't have to worry about them anymore.' She told me she had gone to the table where the football players sat and told them about the bullies. She said to them that if they wanted their driver's license approval from her daddy, she'd need them to help us."

"What did the players do?" Barb said.

"Tina said they took the bullies behind the cafeteria to let them know that if they wanted to have their driver's licenses when they got up to high school, and if they didn't want to have a busted nose or lip or broken bone, they should *not* tease or mock or bully her or me *ever* again. So I guess the moral of the story is, 'It's not just what you know, but who you know.'"

Barb reached across the table and put her hand on Kate's arm. "It sounds like the Lord protected you. And the moral to *that* story is, 'It's not just who you are, but whose you are.'"

"How did it make you feel to have Tina help like that?" I asked.

Kate beamed. "Loved, Daddy. I mean, I know she's a wonderful friend, a friend that looks for the best in me and gives me her best. But now I know for sure she's my once and for all truest and bestest friend forever and ever."

That led to a terrific discussion that evening about bullying. We discussed how to become a defender of weaker kids, how not to be afraid to stand up for and protect other people being bullied or abused, how and when to stand up to bullies, and when and how to walk away.

Kate and Scott came up with three guiding rules that they would try to practice individually and with their friends. They would (1) not bully others, (2) stand up for victims of bullying by telling someone—one of us, a teacher, a coach, or an administrator—and (3) look out for and befriend those kids who were loners or outcasts. Kate also suggested that we, as a family, pray for victims of bullying and even for the bullies.

That night as I said a bedtime prayer with Kate, she quipped, "Daddy, I've made a decision."

"What's that?"

"I'm done being a victim of cerebral palsy. I'm not going to let other people's views of me define me or my life."

"So are *you* going to be the person who defines you?" I asked.

Kate shook her head. "Nope. The person who will tell me my value, my role, and who I really am is Jesus. He created me, he designed me, he wove me together in Mom's womb, he knows me, and he loves me. I'm precious and beautiful in his eyes, and he has chosen me to be his daughter, his friend, and his treasured possession. He formed the stars, and he designed me. I think that's all that counts."

I felt tears flowing down my cheeks. "Well, you're precious and beautiful in my eyes also. Does that count?"

She giggled. "Well, of course. After all, I'm the daughter of *a* great physician and *the* Great Physician. What more could a girl want?"

I hugged my sweet girl and sensed Jesus whisper, *"You're blessed when you get your inside world—your mind and heart—put right. Then you can see God in the outside world."*[2]

12

House Fire

It's a long story how we got to this point, but as we began renovating the old house we had bought on Lake Toho, the contractor found so much rot and corrosion behind the walls and under the floors that we were going to have to tear it down and build from the ground up.

After dealing with our initial disappointment, we were excited to find out we could donate the old building to a local volunteer fire department for a controlled burn to train young firefighters and receive a tax deduction, so it turned into a double blessing. After much planning and going through permitting, the day had finally arrived.

Before we could burn down our old home, our contractor harvested most of the serviceable crown and floor molding and the utilizable doors and hardware. For the last few days before the fire, the firefighters had been on site, disconnecting the plumbing, sewer, gas, and electricity. They used chain saws to cut a variety of holes in the floors and through the roof, which would allow them to control the burn one room at a time, from the inside out.

The goal was for all debris to fall toward the center of the house and burn to ash.

The day of the burn, the firefighters arrived before dawn. They preplaced fire hoses around the house to keep the fire suppressed and protect our neighbors' homes on either side. Don Shearer, whom I knew from Rotary Club and who served as a deputy sheriff, arrived with several other deputies to direct traffic on Neptune Road. They also set up a perimeter to keep any curious observers a safe distance away. Don helped erect and organize a command tent to house medics, equipment, and communication gear. A rental service unloaded several porta-potties in our front yard as a tank truck pulled up.

The fire chief hopped out and introduced himself. "Doc, good to meet'cha. Name's Bobby Samuelson. Appreciate you helping out my team and me."

"It's a win-win, Chief."

"Just call me Bobby." He pointed at the tanker. "This carries the foam we're gonna spray on the sides of your neighbors' houses, as well as the plants and trees near your home. It'll not only serve as insulation to protect any item it clings to, but it's biodegradable and easy to wash off after the fire is done."

As we walked around the house, he pointed out a hedge of Ligustrum bushes only eighteen inches from one side of the house. "If'n you don't mind, Doc, as an experiment, I'd like to spray this hedge. I don't think it will protect against a 1,500-to-2,000-degree flame, but it sure won't hurt to try."

As several fire trucks pulled up, neighbors and other curious folks gathered. The Hartmans, Prathers, Sabettos, and several friends from the Rotary Club set up a tent and tables filled with food and refreshments.

Small-town America at its best, I thought. I mentioned that to Jimmy Sabetto. He laughed and said, "The nice thing about living in a small town like Kissimmee is that when you don't know what you're doing, everyone else does! There may be no secrets in Kissimmee, but there are no strangers either."

Bobby approached me. "Doc, we have an extra outfit and breathing apparatus. We'd like you to join us inside for the start of the burn if you're interested."

"I'd love to!" I responded before thinking about it. In moments he had me dressed in a fire suit, boots, a belt and backpack, a two-way communication radio, and an airtight helmet that connected to a breathing container.

As he secured the mask to my outer fire coat, Bobby said, "Once I seal this, no air or smoke or fumes can penetrate the helmet or suit. You're to stay by my side at all times. I'll take you in the house before the burn, and when I say it's time to leave, we'll leave with no questions. Understand?"

I nodded.

"You must inhale forcefully to start the breathing mechanism. Don't panic, but it will take a few seconds to start, okay?"

As he secured the helmet, several firefighters gathered around. My breaths were short and shallow, and I sensed no fresh air. It was getting hot inside, and I attempted to take a deep breath. There was *no* air! I tried again and again. Nothing. I was suffocating and sensed an overwhelming panic was building. But I didn't want to show any fear or hesitancy in front of the team. I tried once more, with no success. Just as I was about to rip off the helmet, they all started laughing. Bobby reached behind me, turned a valve, and a rush of cool, fresh air filled my helmet. My terror subsided as I inhaled several deep breaths.

Through my helmet speaker, I heard Bobby chuckling. "That was just an initiation ritual, Doc. That's why so many gathered around. We've all been through it, but you did much better than most rookies. Welcome to our team. Let's go!"

We walked to the back of the house and into our former living/ dining room. In one corner was a three-to-four-foot pile of kindling with a one-to-two-foot hole in the ceiling above it. A pair of two-person teams entered, one on each side of us.

"Each team includes an experienced firefighter and a rookie,"

Bobby told me. "You'll be learning the same way they are by watching your first controlled burn. Let's squat down."

We did, and he continued explaining. "Once the fire begins, this room will fill with super-heated fumes that will increase to 1,200 to 1,400 degrees Fahrenheit. Anyone who stands and sticks their head and shoulders into it will instantly fry. But if you follow my every command immediately, without question, and to the letter, you'll be safe. Agreed?"

I nodded.

"I need to hear from you."

"Yes, sir!"

"Here we go. They will light the kindling. It has a fire accelerant. Remember to stay down."

I nodded. One of the firefighters lit the kindling and the fire began to grow.

"Notice her body," Bobby said as the fire grew to resemble a large candle flame, three feet across. "Now, see! She's shaped like an hourglass with her head on top and her hair sucking into the ceiling."

I noticed what looked like a clear, viscous liquid forming on the ceiling and then getting thicker.

"That's the super-heated fumes. Here, give me your hand." He lifted our hands to within a few inches of the undulating cloud. The heat was scalding, even through our super-insulated gloves.

"With modern protective gear like we have on, firefighters no longer have to do what they called 'surround and drown' a fire. We can safely go in and fight her face-to-face. People are always asking me how it is that firefighters run into a burning building when everyone else is running out. The answer is great training, great gear, and great courage."

A loud pop sound from behind startled me.

"That's her first breath," Bobby said. "As she needs more oxygen, she'll suck it in, pulling in the windowpanes, then they'll pop out as she runs out of air, and then it'll repeat. If the glass shatters, our suits will protect us."

Her breathing was horrific and surreal at the same time. The deep bellowing sound was Darth Vader-ish and frightening to my core.

"Watch her! She's starting to grow her arms and hands. They'll spread across the ceiling, and the fingers will flex downward as if she wants to pick you up and pull you into her body to consume you."

His prediction was spot-on. One arm extended out from each side of her body, up to the ceiling, and then out across the room at the junction of the top of the wall and the ceiling. When her arms were ten to twelve feet long, her hands and flickering fingers grew and reached out, flexing and attempting to grasp the super-heated gasses again and again. I heard a scream and turned to my left. One rookie and her escort were quickly crawling out of the room. The sound was horrifying.

"Was she burned?"

Bobby shook his head. "I suspect not. It's just that the beast is super frightening to rookies. Some are called to fight her; others learn in events like today that this is *not* their line of work. We have a saying, 'Heroes are no braver than ordinary people, but they are brave five minutes longer.'"

He looked to our right at the other escort. He and Bobby gave each other a thumbs-up and then flexed their elbows like a baseball umpire would do to call a runner out. "That's our signal to retreat. Let's get you to a safe place and let the other professionals take it from here."

When we got to the front of the house, the female firefighter who had left was sitting on a curb, bawling her eyes out. Two firefighters and a medic attempted to comfort her.

When my gloves were off, Bobby had me feel my outer coat. It was almost too hot to touch. As I peeled the layers off, I found my T-shirt, shorts, and undergarments soaked with sweat. I don't think it was the heat—I think it was from utter fear. Every citizen should see what I had been privileged to witness. To have the slightest clue of what these brave men and women face daily increased my admiration and appreciation of what they do and who they are.

Back at the command center, Bobby showed me his console. It had a blueprint of our house drawn onto plexiglass, with little blinking lights of various colors in and around the house. "Each one of these represents one of my people," he said. "If I need to find someone, I can quickly locate them."

Room by room, the house burned. Each room would almost explode into a white-hot flame that would outline the studs and trusses as the wall coverings burned first. When the structural beams burned, the room would collapse. The rooms with the most rot damage burned the quickest, as they had so few studs!

A black plume of smoke rose and blew over Lake Toho. Because the wind was blowing across the lake, there were very few unpleasant odors, but the fire's snapping and crackling was constant. Bobby kept his personnel rotating and well-hydrated. Our family and friends kept them well-fed. The atmosphere was festive and family-like. The firefighters were exceptional professionals, but at the same time, they clearly enjoyed their work.

By early afternoon, only a two-room wing remained. Bobby tapped my shoulder and pointed toward it. "The exterior siding is burning away. See those shingles showing up underneath? That's the old asbestos siding. We were *not* expecting that. Normally, I'd have to douse the burn so that a mitigation company could remove it, but with a burn temperature of 2,000 degrees and with the smoke blowing over the lake, I can just let it combust."

As the burn finished, a pile of glowing ash was all that remained. The skill of these men and women was astounding.

"We'll leave one crew here to monitor the ash for a few hours and douse any flare-ups," Bobby said. "But first, let me show you something. Come, take a walk with me." We headed toward one of our neighbor's houses as the crew used a fire hose to wash off the protective foam. The side of the house was pristine. It was the same for the neighbor's home on the other side and the massive oak that stood next to the back deck—all were burn-free.

"But most amazing of all," he said, pointing to our Ligustrum hedge, "the foam protected the plants, and they were less than two feet from the fire. I'd say it worked pretty well."

"Does it ever get routine, Bobby? Does the grab-your-heart fear I felt today ever go away? Or even diminish?"

He thought a moment as he looked over the smoking ruins and shook his head. "Being fearless isn't possible. In fact, if being brave is the absence of fear, I've never worked with a brave person. All firefighters are frightened—and the more experienced they are, the more frightening this work can be. But I expect my men and women to learn how to control their fear. I demand courage from them—the ability to carry on despite fear. Never-ending instruction, strict discipline, and the three *selfs*—self-respect, self-confidence, and self-control—are foundational for us. These and the necessity of saving lives and livelihoods allows my people to suppress any fear of what we're prepared to accomplish each and every day."

He paused to take a deep breath. "In firefighting school, an older chief told me something that a Greek general said. I never forgot it. 'The bravest are those who have the clearest vision of what is before them, glory and danger alike, and yet notwithstanding, go out to meet it.'"[1]

Bobby scratched the stubble on his chin as he let out a sigh. "I tell my trainees that true courage is being afraid but doing your job anyhow. Bravery is executing your duties with excellence and competence even when scared half to death. For us, purpose leads to the courage that allows us to be resolute and, more times than not, thank God that we are as successful as we were today."

I could only nod in astonishment and appreciation. Even to this day, nothing makes my heart palpitate, or my compassion and concern rise more quickly than the sound of a fire engine screaming by. On board are firefighters, every one of whom will attack their enemy without flinching despite the incredible stress and demands placed upon them. First responders—whether police, firefighters, or EMTs—every one of them are modern-day heroes in our homeland. They have my utter respect and admiration.

13

A New Trick

I BELIEVE GOD GENUINELY DELIGHTS IN CHILDREN. They can be such a blessing—filled with joy, wonder, and laughter. Their trust and innocence so enthralled Jesus that he interacted joyfully with them.

One day some parents brought their children to Jesus. They wanted him to touch and bless their kids, but the disciples scolded them for bothering Jesus. Fortunately, the Master saw what was happening and fussed at his friends.

He said, "Let the children come to me. Don't stop them! For the Kingdom of God belongs to those who are like these children. I tell you the truth, anyone who doesn't receive the Kingdom of God like a child will never enter it."[1]

Then something unique happened. Jesus gathered up all of the kids in his arms, placed his hands on their heads, and blessed each one of them.

I love caring for children from conception to adulthood. I revel in praying for and with them.

It wasn't uncommon for me to walk into the exam room and find an uncomfortable little boy with a BB-sized object up his nostril. Foreign objects in the nose can be quite painful and even more uncomfortable to extract. Therefore, physicians who care for children must employ methods that they can use to remove them. The longer the object stays lodged, the more likely the tender nasal tissue will swell and bleed as the mucosa becomes angrier, more irritated, and gradually distended. The child's snowballing wails can intensify the alarm and panicky feelings of the parent, nurse, and, yes, even the doctor.

The first extraction method I became comfortable using was applying a small drop of superglue to the end of a cotton-tipped applicator. I'd then touch it to the foreign body for a few seconds, giving the seal time to harden. Then the applicator with the foreign body attached could be pulled out painlessly. If the patient was cooperative, the procedure was quick and easy for all. The obvious disadvantage of this method is that care must be taken to see that the applicator does not touch and stick to the mucous membranes, making a painful situation worse.

For items that have been in the nose for a while, however, the foreign body can cause an infection in the surrounding tissues so that it can't often be seen because there's too much swelling or it's too far back in the child's nose. In those cases, I would quickly dislodge the offender by passing a pediatric catheter down the child's nostril and pushing the foreign body into the throat. The kiddos have a strong enough gag reflex that prevents them from aspirating it into their lungs.

It was a grandmother from a pioneer family, Connie Partin, who taught me what became my favorite method. It all happened when I saw one of her many grandsons, a toddler who sat calmly in his mother's lap. He had pushed a pea-sized bean up one of his nostrils. I should point out that almost all of these cases involve little boys. Very few are little girls since they seem to have an innate aptitude to avoid sticking objects into their noses. For boys, the practice of sticking things up their noses seems to be as natural as breathing.

I had made the diagnosis, and as one of our nurses, Judy, was finding the superglue and an applicator, Connie entered the room. After appraising the situation, she looked at me. "Do you mind if I try an old trick?" she asked. "It's always worked for my boys."

Since I always enjoyed learning, I nodded and had a seat. She then took the little one and laid him on the exam table as Judy reentered the exam room. We both watched as Connie softly cooed to the little boy, leaned over, took a deep breath, covered his mouth with hers, and quickly exhaled—just as if she was giving him mouth-to-mouth resuscitation.

To all of our amazement, the offending bean blew out of the boy's nose, glancing off Connie's cheek and landing on the exam table. I'm not sure whose eyes were wider: the little boy's or mine.

From that day on, I used that method—well, usually I had the parent do it. Most succeeded on the first try. And wouldn't you know it, I don't remember ever having a repeat customer. Wisdom often comes from hands-on experience. Unfortunately for boys, these wisdom-building experiences all too often involve bad choices!

Another day, I had a little kiddo who had stuck a pencil in his ear. Note the gender? Fortunately, he put in the eraser end; unfortunately, the eraser broke off. It worried me that it would be hard to remove and I might have to send the family to an ENT doctor up in Orlando. We were fortunate that Tom Blain, DDS, the dean of the dentists in our town, was in the office visiting with John. As I presented the case to John, Tom said, "Want me to show you an easy way to get it out?"

I was game. Tom said, "Give me a few minutes. I'll run over to my office and be right back."

He returned and showed us an instrument with two small tubes connected by a small handheld pump device that emptied into a single nipple.

"These two tubes contain semifluid dental impression materials," Tom explained. "When they come out of the dispensing tip, they mix and quickly harden into a soft gel-like substance that doesn't pull apart. I've used this with the docs around here for years. If you and the mother want, I'll gently inject it into the child's external auditory canal, let it harden for a few minutes, and hopefully we can remove it with the foreign body attached. The technique is quick, easy, painless, and a far more pleasant experience for the child and the doctor than any other I know of."

John, the mom, Judy, and I were all *very* interested; the child not as much since he was having some ear pain. Nevertheless, the youngster was surprisingly cooperative as Dr. Blain filled his ear canal with the substance, leaving a clump outside the ear to create a "handle" to pull on.

After fifteen minutes, Dr. Blain and I reentered the room. Tom had the little boy sit in his mother's lap, and he surprised us all by saying to the toddler, "You put it in, so you pull it out." He guided the little guy's hand up to the ear, and we all laughed, including the tiny tot, as he pulled out the impression material with the offending eraser attached.

Tom loved teaching us "new dogs" his "old trick."

The next week, a mother brought her four-year-old son to the office, concerned he could not hear anymore. This child had always been most friendly and full of life, but today he seemed somewhat somber. During my exam, I saw clumps of rock-hard earwax in both of the child's ears. Using Dr. Blain's technique, both plugs were quickly and easily removed.

As the little boy and his mom were preparing to leave, the youngster, back to his more usual state of exuberance, started to sprint out of the room toward the nurses' station to choose a reward sticker. His mother calmly scolded, "Not so fast!"

The child promptly turned around with eyes widened and exclaimed, "Mommy, I can hear you!"

I could almost hear Jesus's voice, in a whisper, saying to me, *"Anyone who welcomes a little child like this on my behalf is welcoming me."*[2]

14

Table Fellowship

CONSTRUCTION OF OUR BRAND-NEW LAKESIDE HOME went quickly with no significant complications. Moving-in day was a joyous day. Friends, new neighbors, staff from the office, and some of my favorite patients spent the entire day loading their trucks and cars as we moved load after load of boxes and furniture into the new house. Food and fellowship, labor and laughter, along with appreciation and affection, were hallmarks of the day—capped off by Pastor Pete leading a prayer of blessing, thanksgiving, and dedication over the house.

After everyone left, Barb, Kate, Scott, and I slowly walked from room to room. The French Creole cottage architecture reminded us of houses from our hometown of Baton Rouge. The hardwood floors were brightened by the sunset reflecting off the lake and streaking through the expansive floor-to-ceiling windows. The large back deck was bordered by massive old oak trees, a small but lovely orchid greenhouse, and a rear lawn of lush St. Augustine grass that extended to the lakeshore and our now-renovated dock that reached into Lake Toho and from which we could watch glorious sunsets over historic downtown Kissimmee.

After the kids were asleep, Barb and I finished some final work in the kitchen. "I love everything about our new house. But I think I most appreciate the breakfast nook here in the kitchen. I think we'll be having almost all of our family meals here."

"Except those we have on our boat out on the lake!" I said.

"What boat?" Barb asked.

"The one you're going to let me buy."

Barb laughed. "Don't hold your breath, big boy!"

An eternally significant dinner discussion began with Scott saying, "Dad, I think it's time."

"For what?"

"You, Mom, and Kate always talk about having Jesus in your life. Y'all talk about him *all* the time. You pray and you read the Bible."

Scott, a sixth grader at the time, looked directly at Barb. "Mom, when you and Kate were deciding to get baptized a few years back, I listened to you talking about that. I was so happy when the pastor let Daddy baptize you both at the same service. I knew I wasn't ready back then. Since then, I know I've not always made y'all proud, and I've not always made the best decisions. But I've been thinking about it, and I think I'd like to ask Jesus to come into my life."

Barb and I looked at each other, broad smiles on our faces.

"That's awesome to hear, Scott. We're so pleased," Barb said.

We talked about what that decision meant as a family, and after dinner, he and I took Kate to a gymnastics class. While we sat on a mat at the gym, we continued to talk about his decision. "Scott, the Bible says that God knew you and formed you before you were born. He loves you more than you can ever imagine, and he wants to have a personal relationship with you. But you, Kate, Mom, and I—and every person, for that matter—have made bad choices and mistakes. Because of this, we've separated ourselves from God and can't know him firsthand. That separation leaves a God-shaped hole in each of our hearts that we can't fill. Maybe that's what you're feeling?"

He nodded.

"I remember feeling the same way in college, bud. That's where I first learned that the Bible tells us Jesus is God's provision for filling that emptiness in our hearts. Beginning a personal relationship with Jesus allows us to experience God's love.[1] I once heard someone say, 'The greatest gift ever offered to each of us is God's love, and the greatest tragedy is not to accept it—to leave the gift unopened.'"

Scott asked questions, and we discussed them. Then I said, "I remember when I decided to accept Christ's sacrifice for my wrongdoing and to trust him as my Savior and Lord."

I pulled a small New Testament out of my pocket and opened it. "Back then, this verse meant a lot to me. Jesus says, 'Look at me. I stand at the door. I knock. If you hear me call and open the door, I'll come right in.'[2] So I invited him in, and my life's never been the same."

Scott looked up at me and nodded. "Daddy, that's what I want."

My heart filled with joy. "Want to say a prayer with me?"

He nodded, I put the Bible down, and we held hands. I prayed, and he repeated after me: "Jesus, I want to have a personal forever friendship with you. Thank you for dying on the cross for my sins. I open my heart and the door of my life and invite you to come in. Thank you for forgiving me of my sins and giving me eternal life that starts right now. I want you to make me the kind of person you want me to be. Amen."

Scott reached up and gave me a long, hard hug. As we embraced, I said, "Scott, the Bible says that everyone who believes in Jesus and has accepted him becomes a child of God. So, what are you now?"

He sat back and thought a moment as he looked across the gym. Then a smile spread across his face. "I'm a child of God?"

"That's right. And if you're a child of God, and so am I, then what are we?"

He smiled ear to ear. "Brothers!" he exclaimed as we hugged again.

The next evening, we celebrated Scott's spiritual birth over a special dinner. And at subsequent dinners, we discussed things we had learned from the Bible about baptism.

One evening, Scott announced, "Dad, I want you to baptize me, just like you did for Mom and Kate." He smiled at them. "My sisters!"

Over the years we learned that a healthy, well-knit family almost always had well-worn seats at the dinner table. I liked Scott's observation that, "When we eat together as a family, food just tastes better." Or, as we once heard someone pray before dinner, "Lord, bless the food before us, the family beside us, and the love between us."

It was pretty easy to say "Amen" to that!

———

A couple of days after Scott's life- and eternity-changing decision, I spent some time journaling about how spiritual fellowship seems so much richer when it occurs during an unrushed meal. It struck me that the dining table is an icon or a symbol of God's grace and goodness—that to sit and commune with people over a meal is to occupy a remarkable, even sacred, space.

I never forgot a great quote I once heard: "Small minds discuss people. Average minds discuss events. Great minds discuss ideas."[3] I loved discussing big ideas and things that mattered with Barb and my children at our dinner table.

I also remembered that Jesus used mealtimes to interact with his disciples, followers, and some pretty disrespectable folks, which led the religious hypocrites to call him "a friend of tax collectors and sinners."[4] He talked with, taught, and loved on folks over shared meals. He told and listened to stories. They experienced laughter and joy while sharing sadness and tears.

At mealtime, my family and friends can rejoice in where we've been and what we've learned while together dreaming of where we might go one day. We can pray together at the table. Over a meal, we can collectively experience and share God's nearness, kindness, and love. No wonder Jesus taught, "For where two or three gather in my name, there am I with them."[5] He loves mealtimes and has promised us that when he returns, we'll dine together at a spectacular banquet![6]

Biologists say that sharing fellowship over a meal at a table is uniquely human; no other creature eats at a table. So it makes sense that there's more to food than fuel—or that there should be. To be truly human is to understand that we don't consume food only for sustenance. No wonder the Passover meal, the Last Supper, and Holy Communion all center on a family table. And when the prophets predicted the day when God's kingdom would arrive, they all described a magnificent feast. Isaiah predicted the day when "the LORD Almighty will prepare a feast of rich food for all peoples, a banquet of aged wine—the best of meats and the finest of wines."[7]

I was so blessed to be learning the art of an unhurried meal around a table with my family and the people I loved during our days in Kissimmee. Although not listed as one of the classical "spiritual disciplines," I believe "table fellowship" should be. Around the table I learned that real life includes the gift of mealtime fellowship with loving family and friends.

15

Faith and Medicine

ONE MORNING, JOHN AND I were, as was our almost daily habit, sharing coffee and the latest gossip . . . er, news . . . before starting our office hours. He was quiet for a few seconds, taking a slow sip of coffee, before he looked at me.

"Walt," he said, "I've been considering something. How come we don't share our faith in the office with more of our patients? I mean, we're both active in our churches, on short-term missions, and in other ministries. We both pray with folks occasionally. We discuss spiritual and religious issues with patients when the situation warrants it, especially in critical or end-of-life situations. Still, we don't routinely bring our faith to work on a day-to-day basis, do we?"

That discussion was an epiphany moment for us both and made perfect sense. Medicine, of almost all vocations, is the ideal intersection between profession and spirituality. When folks get sick, they nearly always begin considering spiritual things like God, faith, prayer, and eternity. Many wonder if God is punishing them, doesn't love them, or has abandoned them when they become severely ill. Others ponder where God is in their illness and what he's planning to show or teach them. With that as a backdrop, John and I decided to explore the idea of more intentionally incorporating our faith into our daily practice.

I shared our idea over my next breakfast with Pastor Pete. Besides being an experienced clergyman, he served as the fire department chaplain and was on the hospital board of directors. I knew his advice would be invaluable. When he heard me outline our idea, he could not have been more encouraging.

"There is a distance between the pulpit and the pew that does not exist at the patient's bedside," he said. "Think about it, Walt. The average physician sees more spiritually seeking people in a day than the typical minister does in a month."

Pastor Pete took a bite of his hash browns. "But I recommend you always introduce spiritual topics or interventions like a prayer—with respect, with sensitivity, and with the patient's permission. You knock on their spiritual door, but let them be the one to open it and invite you in."

Pete reminded me of one of my medical school professors who profoundly influenced my early understanding of the intersection of faith and medicine. Paul Brand, MD, was a world-famous medical missionary and hand surgeon for lepers. When he served at the national leprosarium in Carville, Louisiana, about seventy miles upriver from New Orleans, I was privileged to spend a medical school rotation with him.

Dr. Brand emphasized that my primary responsibility to patients, even as a faithful physician, was not to meet a patient's spiritual needs. Instead, he stressed that I needed first to combine competence, character, and compassion. He taught that Scripture demanded that I was to work in my day-to-day practice "with all [my] heart, as working for the Lord, and not for human masters."[1]

"Being a Spirit-filled believer is no excuse for practicing sloppy medicine," Dr. Brand told me. "If you want patients to pay attention to your faith, you must first pay attention to your work." He loved quoting great thinkers, both ancient and modern. More than once, Dr. Brand quoted from Dr. Martin Luther King Jr.'s talk to some students in Philadelphia:

> And when you discover what you will be in your life, set out to do it as if God Almighty called you at this particular moment in history to do it. Don't just set out to do a good job. Set out to do such a good job that the living, the dead, or the unborn couldn't do it any better.
>
> If it falls your lot to be a street sweeper, sweep streets like Michelangelo painted pictures, sweep streets like Beethoven composed music, sweep streets like Leontyne Price sings before the Metropolitan Opera. Sweep streets like Shakespeare wrote poetry. Sweep streets so well that all the hosts of heaven and earth will have to pause and say: Here lived a great street sweeper who swept his job well.[2]

I loved doing rounds with Dr. Brand at the hospital for lepers. He had an almost schoolboyish enthusiasm for each of his patients. His eyes would often mist when they told him how others treated them with hatred, scorn, and rejection; of the psychological pain and genuine suffering they endured; and of the endless trials and tribulations of living with leprosy. He sent me a copy of an article he wrote for Christian health-care professionals in which he wrote:

> In the medical profession, we do have a matchless, wonderful opportunity to meet people at times of their real need, real suffering, real storms. During their distress, they are often ready to open up their hearts and expose their fears and worries and concerns. They will talk about their families and about eternity and the other things bottled up inside them. They are broken and afraid when they face a medical situation. They often are very willing to express these things, and this gives us the opportunity to present the grace of our Lord Jesus Christ.[3]

During rounds, I would marvel at how Dr. Brand would take time with each patient, often sharing a Bible verse or a biblical principle about what bothered them the most.

"How do you know what to share?" I asked him one time.

He thought a moment. "Two ways. Number one, I believe you can't share what you don't have. So God's Word has to permeate your soul, and God's Spirit needs to fill you—needs to control and empower you. With those foundations, you have to be intentional in listening to the often still small voice of Scripture and Spirit. With each patient, I'm praying as I talk to them. I believe that's why the apostle Paul reminds us to 'Rejoice always, pray continually, give thanks in all circumstances; for this is God's will for you in Christ Jesus. Do not quench the Spirit.'[4]

"The second factor for me," he went on, "is to listen to the patients—really listen. If I clarify that I'm serving God as I care for them, and he has sparked an interest in himself in them, they'll pick up on that and, as I am seeing them, they'll bring it up. They'll ask a question or two. In fact, if your patients are not asking about your faith, then I must wonder if you've not hidden your light under a basket.

"And I find it important to remember that it's God, not me, who must spark a flame of interest or longing in himself in my patients. Our job as Christians called into health care is to meet and love our patients where they are on their spiritual journey and to both serve and love them the best we can."

I was most deeply touched by Dr. Brand's stories of myriad individual patients he'd treated over the years, particularly during his time in India, where he came face-to-face with the "untouchables" in India's pernicious caste system. Even though these patients were considered the "nobodies" in Indian society, Dr. Brand touched, hugged, prayed for, and wept with them. "Walt, all of our patients are created in the image of God," he said. "We must always honor and respect that image."

Dr. Brand's example and teaching formed a healthy foundation for me in my early years in medicine, but unfortunately, it was one from which I had wandered. I shared that with my partner that morning over coffee.

"John, after medical school, I was so excited about everything Dr. Brand taught me about bringing faith into patient care," I said, "but during residency and my early practice days, the storms of life intervened and rudely interrupted. Kate's diagnosis of cerebral palsy nearly wrecked my faith in God and my marriage. Then I chose to leave God on the sidelines while in my residency at Duke. So, your challenge about our not bringing our faith to work on a day-to-day basis was convicting to the max."

"For me too, partner. But maybe the difficulties we've both experienced in the past—the struggles and strains our families and we have gone through—are God's way of setting himself as a foundation for both of us. Maybe now we're ready to dedicate ourselves, our families, and our practice to him."

That night, after the kids were settled, I shared with Barb what John and I had discussed. After hearing me out, Barb said, "I think John's right." Then she reached over to her Bible and opened it.

"I read this passage this morning in The Message version." Her fingers took her to the right verse. "Consider it a sheer gift, friends, when tests and challenges come at you from all sides. You know that under pressure, your faith-life is forced into the open and shows its true colors. So don't try to get out of anything prematurely. Let it do its work, so you become mature and well-developed, not deficient in any way."[5]

She closed the book. "Here's what I take from this passage. Our past and future storms are actually a gift from God. So, let's let them go to work."

"Amen," I said, hugging her close.

I didn't know it then, but the Lord was beginning to set up a series of divine appointments where he would start to teach me of the hope, health, and healing that only he can bring through various trials, troubles, and tribulations.

PART TWO
God's in Every Storm

Life isn't about waiting for the storm to pass.
It's about learning how to dance in the rain.

Vivian Greene, twentieth-century
British author

16

Life-Giving Hope

HOPE QUENCHED IS FATAL, for when hope dies, so does the heart and life itself is quickly extinguished. The Bible tells us that hope gives us endurance,[1] and, according to an ancient proverb, "Hope deferred makes the heart sick, but a dream fulfilled is a tree of life."[2] It's been said that hope is like a star, seen best on the darkest of nights. I remember a shiny example of hope's truth, power, and healing in a patient of mine named Eva.

Eva became addicted to tobacco as a preteen. Everyone she knew—her parents, relatives, and every single friend at school—smoked. By the time I met her, sixty years of smoking more than a pack a day had ravaged her body, especially her lungs, leading to severe emphysema. Several other chronic medical conditions affected her health, but lung disease was the worst and in its last stages. There was little I could do other than keep her comfortable.

As her lung condition worsened, we started planning for the fast-approaching end of her life, despite the best possible medical care. Those discussions are never easy between a physician and a patient. But as the reality of her passing approached, she, like many who are terminally ill, came to accept and perhaps even welcome the end of her suffering. What surprised me was that even in the face of death, she wasn't comfortable talking about spiritual things.

"There's a fine line between a long, drawn-out sermon and a hostage situation," she said to me one day, chuckling. Never a regular churchgoer as an adult, Eva described her last visit to her daughter's church in this manner: "After the service, I told the pastor that if I ever returned, I would give him some money. He said, 'Well, thank you very much. But may I ask why?' And I told him he was one of the poorest preachers I'd ever heard."

Comedian Henny Youngman, king of the one-liner, had nothing on Eva. One day she asked me with a gleam in her eye, "Is my last will and testament considered a dead giveaway?"

At another time, she quipped, "I told my daughter that my funeral is *not* to be a grave affair. I want to put the *fun* back in *fun*eral. I don't want folks crying because I'm gone. I want them to smile and laugh because I was here!"

My favorite of Eva's statements to me is this: "I never wanted to live forever, but I wanted to create something that would survive me. My kids are exactly that."

Predicting death's arrival is difficult for physicians. We may forecast that the Angel of Death will appear in a week or two, but it's a pleasant surprise when the Grim Reaper doesn't show up as predicted. At other times, we're sure years remain, only to watch in shock as the Divine Messenger appears far sooner than expected.

In Eva's situation, it seemed as though the end was coming quickly. She was on round-the-clock oxygen. Her muscles atrophied. She wasn't able to walk or carry out her daily living activities without a walker and the help of one or two people. She slept for lengthy periods of each day. As the end drew close, she decided not to die at home.

"I don't want the kids walking into this house after I'm gone and thinking of me like this! When I become but a memory, I want it to be a good one."

She chuckled as she shared another witticism: "My momma used to say, 'Death leaves a heartache no other can heal; love leaves memories no one can steal.'"

Following her wishes, I admitted her to the hospital, and almost by the hour, she dwindled. I explained to Eva and her grieving family that I could prolong her life a little longer if I put her on a ventilator. Given the likelihood she'd never come off it and breathe on her own, she declined that option. As a result, she began the rapid journey toward the inevitable, lapsing into a coma as the carbon dioxide in her system rose to toxic levels.

Her loved ones stayed close. I believe that patients in a coma can hear conversations around them; therefore, I encouraged those caring for and visiting Eva to touch, talk to, pray with, and even hug her. They all readily complied.

During morning rounds one day, Abigail, Eva's daughter, asked me to step into the hallway. Abby and her family were also patients of mine. Just the day before, I had performed Abby's prenatal ultrasound, finding a healthy baby girl, so I suspected she had a question about that.

"Dr. Walt," she began, "Momma always wanted to be a grandmother. We didn't tell her about this pregnancy because our earlier miscarriage would have been her first grandchild. She took that so hard that we didn't want to tell her about this one until we were sure the baby was likely to make it. Anyway, she doesn't know. Should I tell her or would the news be too depressing for her? I mean, with her not being able to live to see the baby and all?"

Whenever confronted with a conundrum like this, I would say a super quick silent prayer, asking the Lord for wisdom and guidance. I sensed the freedom to advise Abby to share her splendid news with her mother. When she asked me to join her, I felt like it was a privilege to stand by and watch as Abby held Eva's hand and shared the announcement.

"Momma," she said, as tears ran down her cheeks, "Dr. Walt did an ultrasound yesterday because I'm going to have a baby next fall. Yes, Momma, I'm pregnant. I'm sorry you won't be here for her birth, but we'll remember you and talk about you forever."

She squeezed the hand of her unresponsive mother, sniffling and holding back tears. "She would have loved you as much as I do—maybe more. I wish she could meet you, but we'll always tell her about you and how special you were."

Instantly, Eva's eyebrows twitched, and tears formed in the inner recesses of each closed eyelid. Abby's eyes widened, and she whispered, "Dr. Walt, she squeezed my fingers. Do you think she heard me?"

I nodded. "I'm certain of it."

The proof of my certainty materialized later that morning: Eva rallied in a way that stunned her nurses, the consulting pulmonologist, and me. Her breathing improved, and her carbon dioxide levels dropped. The next day, as I sat on her bed and held her hand, she opened her eyes, looked at me, and said, "Good morning!"

I'm sure my smile lit up the entire room. "Eva, I was afraid you'd be leaving us. Welcome back!"

"Why die?" she whispered. "I've got a granddaughter coming. I want to be at her birth."

"Me too," I said.

"I remember the first birth I attended," she said softly. "There's nothing as miraculous as a baby being born. It's wonderful!"

"Tell me about it." I wondered what birth she was referring to.

"I remember that, at first, it was very black, then very light, then I was slapped on the butt and I cried. Of course, I'm referring to my birth!"

It took me a second, then I chuckled.

"But I must disagree with you." I saw an opening, and I was going to pursue it gently.

"About what?"

"I think being born again is even more miraculous than being born."

Her eyes twinkled, and I witnessed the return of their old spark as she smiled. "You sound like a preacher, Doc. Well, if I'm not yet born again spiritually, at least I'm born again physically."

"Welcome back, Eva. Mind if I say a quick prayer of thanks?"

"Only if you don't charge me!"

Her quip reminded me of an old Henny Youngman joke: "A doctor gave a man six months to live. The man couldn't pay his bill, so he gave him another six months."[3]

I didn't tell Eva that joke, of course, but I believed the Lord had given her some extra time to know him. Eugene Peterson, the man responsible for The Message version of the Bible, translated an ancient proverb this way, "Unrelenting disappointment leaves you heartsick, but a sudden good break can turn life around."[4]

Eva was living proof of that truth. So the question became, What would each of us do with that time?

I would soon find out.

17

Born Again and Again

EVA'S STRENGTH INCREASED EVERY DAY as her appetite for food and visitors returned. With the aid of physical therapists and a walker, she was soon up and about. She still required supplemental oxygen, but her will to live rebounded, and within a few days, I was able to discharge her.

From the hospital doors, she walked from the wheelchair to her husband's car without help. Those of us watching applauded Eva and her Creator-healer. Before they drove away, she turned to me and pointed to her plastic wristband. "This is not accurate, Dr. Walt. I thought you should know."

"What's that?"

"It says I'm a fall risk. Well, with all the medical problems I have, I'll have you know that I'm also a winter, spring, and summer risk."

We all laughed as she waved. I wondered if she was booked to do a comedy show at Caesars Palace in Las Vegas.

"Goodbye, sweet hospital!" she proclaimed, smiling and blowing kisses our way. "I'm not coming back!"

When I delivered that precious baby girl about five months later,

Eva served as Abby's doula for the entire labor and as a tearful eyewitness to another miracle of birth. She was radiant as Sandi, who assisted me with the delivery, handed the swaddled baby to Eva, who gleefully held, rocked, and cooed at her first grandchild. Abby beamed as she watched.

"Momma," she said softly. "Meet little Eva. We're naming her after her grandma."

Eva softly sobbed as she rubbed little Eva's cheek. In the future, the two Evas were a delight to observe—always smiling and laughing when they came in together for each other's checkups. I was able to end the visits for them both with prayer, prompting Grandma to ask more and more questions about God and the Bible.

In response I gave her a Bible, which she graciously accepted, and I would write out spiritual prescriptions for her—Bible verses or books to read. I continued to keep her in my prayers as she began taking many ministeps along her spiritual journey.

Our entire team at the practice was working on increasing our spiritual sensitivity. John initiated a morning prayer time with our staff that was well received, and our nurses and doctors would pray for and with patients. It was an exciting time for all involved.

One morning after our prayer time, our physical therapist, Joanne Woida, caught me in the hall. "Do you have time for a wonderful story?"

I nodded.

"Last week, during one of my morning quiet times, I was asking the Lord to use me any way he could. I don't do that every day, but that day I felt impressed to ask that. I drove out to the country to visit a patient at her home. I hadn't seen her before. But I found out the woman had a terminal disease. She was walking around the house and seemed to be doing well. We sat to talk, and she wanted to talk about eternity—about death and the hereafter."

"Did that surprise you?"

"It did since we had never met. So, I asked her if she knew the Lord, and she said, 'Oh, you speak like my daughter.' She told me about her daughter's belief in Christ. She didn't know a lot about it, so I started telling her about the assurance of heaven that Christ will give you when you turn your heart over to him and how a friend of mine had done that and how I know today she is in heaven. Then you know what happened?"

I shook my head.

"She said, 'Can I know him now?'" Joanne laughed. "It floored me. I mean, you want to be prepared. You want to share with people, but when they respond so fast, sometimes you're shocked—taken aback."

"So, what happened? What did you do?" I asked.

"I asked her if she had a Bible, and she did. Believe it or not, she said her doctor gave it to her. Anyway, we went over some Scripture, and she perked up when I shared where it says, 'Whoever has the Son has life; whoever does not have the Son of God does not have life. I write these things to you who believe in the name of the Son of God so that you may know that you have eternal life.'[1] That's when I prayed with her, and she asked for forgiveness and turned her heart over to God."

"Amazing! That is a wonderful story!"

"She was so excited. And then she asked me, 'Am I born again?' I turned to the Gospel of John and read about Jesus's discussion with Nicodemus, where he told him, 'Very truly I tell you, no one can see the kingdom of God unless they are born again. . . . Flesh gives birth to flesh, but the Spirit gives birth to spirit. You should not be surprised at my saying, "You must be born again."'[2]

"Then I read the verses where John wrote of Jesus, 'To all who did receive him, to those who believed in his name, he gave the right to become children of God—children born not of natural descent, nor of human decision or a husband's will, but born of God.'[3]

"'So yes, you are born again,' I told her. 'You are now a child of God, and you can know you have eternal life starting this minute!' She got even more excited."

I smiled. "What did she do?"

"She grabbed both of my hands and said, 'So I'm going to heaven when I die?' So I quoted 1 John again. 'I write these things to you who believe in the name of the Son of God so that you may know that you have eternal life.'"[4]

Joanne laughed. "She wanted to go right out and tell her husband and call her children. After we completed the treatment, I went home. I couldn't wait to go back and see her and even thought about inviting her and her husband to come to church with me. But I got a call canceling her next appointment, and then I read her obituary in the paper today. I didn't realize she was that ill." Her eyes misted. "But God knew. So that was a divine appointment. I mean, I rarely do that, but the Holy Spirit clearly directed me to share with her that day."

"Sounds like it was amazing."

Joanne nodded her head and whispered, "It was. That's why I thought you might want to see this." She was holding a stack of papers with a folded-over newspaper on top. She found the obituary page.

I felt my jaw drop and my breath suck in when I saw the obituary that Joanne was pointing to. What I saw were Eva's name and picture.

Speechless for a moment, I could only mutter, "Last week, she was here for her granddaughter's one-year well-baby check. We prayed together for little Eva, and as we were leaving the exam room, she turned and said, 'I'm eternally grateful you are my doctor.' That took me aback. I think I stammered something like, 'Well, thanks.' Then she said, 'At my age, I've learned we should always leave the ones we love with loving words. After all, it may be the last time we see them.' Then she laughed and said, 'Ah, don't worry, Doc! You're gonna be stuck with me for a while! My mother used to say, "Those we love don't go away, they walk beside us every day." Can't get rid of me that easy!'"

I felt my lips quiver as Joanne and I embraced.

I joined baby Eva and Abby at Grandma Eva's *fun*eral, which was a celebration of a life rescued, a testament to the miraculous power of both hope and prayer. I remember the pastor saying, "Some say, 'Life is short, better enjoy it.' But how about, 'Eternity is long, better prepare for it.' A theme of Jesus's teachings is that we are to be prepared. Of course, we are to be prepared for death and eternal life, but in the meantime, we are also to be prepared to live. You don't want to miss a moment of it—your life—because life is so precious and it's so fleeting. Eva was given a new lease on life, and I think she'd say to each of us, 'Are you prepared to live—starting today?'"

The inspirational memorial service was a reminder to me that it's never too late, that your story is never over until it's over, that resurrection and redemption can occur in every life on any day.

You might wonder if stories like this are uncommon, but for most family physicians, they are not rare at all. We never tire of witnessing the impact of hope, dreams, and a firm sense of destiny on a patient's health—and on the living of life itself.

In Eva's case, she had been given a new lease on physical life in order to have another chance at gaining spiritual life for eternity. She experienced the unique miracle of being born again and again—once physically and a second time spiritually. Eva was the most vivid example in all my years of practice that to live with true hope is to be truly alive.

Our hope in eternal life with Jesus is an anchor for our souls during the inevitable storms of life. Despite them, even in their ferocity, and even if they do not calm, we can be sure our Creator will steadily and surely pull us into his final safe and secure harbor.

18

The Missing Link

As John and I considered how to bring our faith into the exam room with most of our patients, we began to explore what others were doing in medical ministry around the country. We didn't find many examples, but we found a few. Some were attractive and some not so much. And, we worried, even if we learned how to minister better, what would that do to our busy schedules?

For example, some who taught medical ministry in those days would encourage believers to confront non-Christians with questions like, "If you were to die tonight, do you know where you'd spend eternity?"

To us, that approach did not seem like a wise, kind, or sensible thing to say to someone sick or in the hospital. When I voiced my thoughts and concerns about this to Bill, he said something I've never forgotten: "Walt, I think the biblical model teaches that our job is not to bring people to Christ, but to bring Christ to people and see where we fit in God's plan for that person."

"I've not heard that before," I responded. We were discussing the matter during one of our weekly breakfasts.

"Well, think about it. The Bible uses words like *cultivation*, *sowing*, and *harvesting* to describe a process of evangelism. It's important to understand that sharing God's Good News is not an event but typically a journey, and one that involves many people influencing the life of each pre-believer with whom they interact. In the cultivation phase of evangelism, people don't trust Christ; they just need to trust a Christian in this stage. As we sow, they learn to trust the Bible and prayer as it relates to problems or concerns they have. Then, at the end of this progression, there's the harvest, where they place their trust in Christ. It can be a lengthy process, with many ministeps that people make toward the Lord as he calls and draws them into a relationship with himself. Make sense?"

As was his habit, Bill pulled out his Bible and flipped through the pages. "Here it is. Paul wrote, 'I planted the seed, Apollos watered it, but God has been making it grow. So neither the one who plants nor the one who waters is anything, but only God, who makes things grow.'"[1] He continued, "Jesus said, 'You're not in charge here. The Father who sent me is in charge. He draws people to me—that's the only way you'll ever come. Only then do I do my work, putting people together, setting them on their feet.'"[2]

I felt a huge weight fall off my shoulders. "Bill, that means I just need to do what God calls me to do, and he'll do his job, right?"

"Yes, and it has helped me to understand that God will normally use one or two dozen Christians in the life of each person he's calling. You don't have to be all of them, you only have to be one of them—using your gifts, talents, and training to serve them. You're not the only link between them and a relationship with God," he told me. "You just don't want to miss a blessing by being a missing link."

I was, as usual, scribbling notes as fast as I could. I knew I needed some time to meditate upon and pray about this conversation. "So, drawing folks to himself is a process that he's actually in charge of, right?"

"Yup. It's not *our* process. It's *his*. It's not our way, it's Yahweh, as I always say. God's already doing his work in their lives. Our job is just to discover where he's active and join him there. Find where he's lit a spark and only fan the flame a little."

"Wow. It's no different than how I care for patients, in the sense that I meet each one right where they are in their life journey. I identify their health needs and desires by taking a history and performing an exam, perhaps with some tests thrown in, and then suggest ways to partner with them to approach, treat, or heal those issues."

"I can imagine," Bill observed, "that each case is different, and each one requires a unique treatment, no matter the illness, correct?"

"Absolutely."

"So now, your job and John's job is to figure out how to bring your faith into the exam room with each patient."

"With *each* patient?" I asked. I'm sure I looked skeptical.

He smiled and flipped open his Bible. "Here it is. Paul's writing again: 'Be wise in the way you act toward outsiders; make the most of every opportunity.'"[3]

Bill looked up from the Good Book. "Imagine the impact in your practice if the word *opportunity* meant an *appointment* or a *consultation*?"

My mind was racing, imagining the implications, but Bill read on. "The verse also says, 'Let your conversation be always full of grace, seasoned with salt.'"[4]

He looked at me and asked, "Do you know what the Greek word that is translated *always* literally means?"

I shook my head. "I do not."

Bill smiled. "It means 'always.'" He laughed. "Walt, every interaction, every appointment, and every visit with every patient can be part of your ministry in medicine."

I felt like I was drowning in a tsunami of spiritual wisdom.

"There's one other thought to ponder," he said. "When you get to the office this morning, what time is your first appointment?"

"Nine o'clock."

"When was that appointment made?"

"I'm not sure. Maybe a week ago, maybe a few weeks or months ago. It varies."

"That's not correct."

His comment confused me. *Where is he going with this?*

"How so?" I asked.

"As we've talked about before, God is sovereign. He's aware of everything in our lives. Could it be that God conceived and designed your first appointment today before time began? Could it be that it's not just a medical appointment but a divine appointment? Most people discount the everyday ordinary in our lives. We forget that God is just as likely to do his work in and through us when we are running an errand, doing a chore, working at our job, talking to a neighbor, or having coffee with a friend as he is when we are having a quiet time or engrossed in some spiritual endeavor or ministry.

"The challenge is for us to be intentional in paying attention, having our spiritual antennas up at all times, so to speak. In the everyday muck of our daily lives, we need to look for the pearls God has prepared for us—where he's prepared to speak or act if we'll just look and listen."

"Bill, what I hear you saying is that I need to be more intentional in recognizing God's movement in my daily, humdrum routine."

"Exactly. The life as a follower of Jesus is never arbitrary. All that you consider haphazard is nothing less than God's appointed order. The Bible gives us lots of examples of divine appointments occurring as people go about their, as you say, daily and humdrum routines. Like when a young woman drew water from a well,[5] an older man lit incense in the temple,[6] a small group of shepherds sat around a nighttime fire chatting,[7] two fishermen were in their boat preparing their nets,[8] and a tax collector was at work in his booth."[9]

He looked out the window as two businessmen were strolling by. They nodded and waved to a woman walking her golden retriever beside a woman pushing a stroller with a child. "Just like those people, these biblical characters were everyday people going about their so-called *mundane routines* when God broke in, broke through, and took hold. Not only were these folks changed for eternity, but he also used them as change agents for others. And as a result, he changed their world and the world—his world."

He emptied his orange juice and wiped his lips. "Maybe, if we look for and listen to him more often, we'll have fewer ordinary days and more spiritually charged ones. In the muckiness of daily living, we can look for the pearls he brings our way. His Spirit can guide us as we begin to go through each day in the power of the Holy Spirit and leave the results to God."

Once again, Bill's biblical advice would be practice-changing, as well as life- and eternity-changing for me and my patients. Our breakfast together that day turned out to be an important day for me, leading me to approach spiritual care the same way I would physical, emotional, and relational treatments. Sure, I would continue to diagnose and treat, but God would take the burden of physical, emotional, relational, *and* spiritual healing off my shoulders. That was his job.

Somewhere I heard the old saying, "The doctor treats, but God heals." The Bible couldn't make this clearer. God told Moses, "I am the LORD, your healer."[10] He told Isaiah, "I will heal."[11] And he told Jeremiah, "I'll bring you healing, and I'll heal you of your wounds."[12]

My medical black bag contained many diagnostic and treatment tools, but now I needed to think more intentionally about my spiritual black bag. I must confess that idea scared me a bit. I had never been trained to apply spiritual care in each patient interaction.

That evening I journaled,

> To be honest, Lord, if I begin to do these things, will my patients think of me as a sort of spiritual kook masquerading as a respectable

doctor? Or will they begin to recognize I'm a Christian who is a family physician, and that I'm trying to represent the Great Physician who, after all, is the one who brings ultimate healing?

If it was at all possible, I wanted my patients to leave my exam room with the assurance that they were cared about and cared for—not just by my staff and me, but by their Creator, who wanted each of them to experience ultimate healing.

I couldn't wait to see how this would play out.

19

God Said "No"

ONE SATURDAY EVENING, the Hartmans and Judges came over for a barbecue. Bill and John sat with me on the back porch, and Bill said, "Walt, if you wouldn't mind my asking, tell me this: If you had to name one of the most difficult parts of your spiritual journey so far, what would you say it was?"

I didn't even have to think about it. My eyes filled with tears, and my head drooped. This kind man gave me a moment to collect my thoughts, and then I began my story.

"It happened during my internship year in family medicine at Duke. John, you were in your last year of the residency. Barb and I were the proud parents of one of the most beautiful baby girls ever born at Durham County General Hospital." I grinned. "Of course, my observation was totally objective."

John laughed. "I remember. Cleta and I came to visit you all at the hospital. Kate was premature, born four weeks early, but she had a full head of hair. Our girls' hair took months to sprout."

"You may remember," I said, "that when she was three months old, Barb recognized that Kate wasn't developing as she should."

"I do," John replied. "I shared Barb's concerns even though I wasn't your family physician."

I soldiered on. "Doctors' visits and several consultations finally led to a brain scan. Back then, CTs were a new technology. I can remember that morning as if it were yesterday. An elderly and gentle pediatric neurologist, Dr. Reinuart, carried Kate, still sedated, out of the scanner and into the waiting room."

"He was one of the most compassionate attendings we had," John said. "If I remember correctly, he and his wife had adopted several kids with disabilities."

I nodded. "That's right. Well, as Dr. Reinuart placed Kate in my arms, he sat down in front of us and broke the devastating news. He said Kate had cerebral palsy, or CP, and explained that she had an incredible amount of brain damage before birth. The scan revealed that she had very little right brain and less than half of a normal-sized left brain. He told us that Kate would never walk, she would never talk, and she would likely never know God as we did—that she would get bigger, but never better.

"I remember him saying, 'I can help you place her in an institution for children with severe disabilities.' That's what some parents did way back then. 'Or,' he said, 'if you choose not to, then the only treatment is to take her home and love her. Of course, I can arrange her physical and speech therapy, but only you can love her as she needs to be loved.'"

"I can't imagine how you must have felt," Bill said.

The news of Kate's diagnosis first hit me like a large burlap sack of rocks. Barb and I were in shock and had no real tools to process the blow. But like the Old Testament character Job, we had some well-meaning friends who did not give us very good advice.

After she was born, people told us that God did not want our daughter to have a disability, that this was *not* his perfect plan for her. They said her disability and disease were from the devil and that God wanted to heal her. I remember them emphasizing that God can heal *any* illness, and if Barb and I would just pray to him for healing, he *would* heal her. So we began praying for her immediate healing.

When Kate did not improve, it made me start to think that God was not listening—or, at least, not responding. At that point others suggested there were only two reasons God was not answering our prayers and healing Kate: either one or both of us had unconfessed sin in our lives or we were not praying the right way. I remember us pouring our whole hearts into the belief that it would happen. However, Kate's condition still did not change.

Still others told us that our prayer must name and claim Kate's healing in Jesus's name, that our prayers would need to rebuke and reprimand Satan and ban him and his angels from our home, and that we must pray, believing and thanking God for the healing *he* would perform on our and Kate's behalf.

When Kate's condition remained unchanged, this comment cut me to the core: "Walt, the problem is *not* God. It's you."

I must admit that I've never been so devastated in my life. I became angry at God for "doing this to me" and for not healing Kate. Day by day, I felt the sky of my life become colder, cloudier, and darker. There was no sunshine. There was no hope. I sank into a deep trough of depression, rage, and resentment. I either could not or would not see that even a silent God is always at work.

One day, in my anger and my shame, with tears running down my cheeks, I lashed out at Barb and screamed, "Kate's CP is your fault!" That's when I abandoned my wife and daughter physically, emotionally, and spiritually. My faith shattered into little pieces. I spent most of my days and nights at the hospital to devote myself to my training. I chose to have an affair with a mistress named Medicine. I left Barb and Kate alone to whatever was coming. My life and emotions hit rock bottom.

We still shared dinner once in a while, but meals were tense. Barb complained bitterly that she was frustrated and afraid because she did not know how to fix us or this situation. She asked me, "Do you think our parents and siblings will love Kate once they know how impaired she is?"

I had no idea and wasn't sure I even cared. I watched from a distance as Barb coped with my abandonment by pouring herself into Kate. She eventually let our parents know but was devastated when my mom told Barb we should bring Kate to her so that my mom could take care of Kate. My mom said, "Before you know it, she'll be walking and talking," which felt like rubbing salt in our wound.

Another night, in her anger and disappointment, Barb said, "I'd have left you and moved home to Baton Rouge if it wasn't for my pride and a lack of resources and a car."

We went through the motions of being married, but we were only roommates with the same last name. There was no forgiveness or grace extended to each other. Selfishness ruled in our hearts, and the Lord was not at the center of our lives anymore. We were cordial to each other, but there was only the most basic communication.

Barb and I were great pretenders. Not one person—not our parents, our siblings, our friends, our church, or anyone at the residency—suspected the depth of our hurt, pain, and unforgiveness toward each other. Things looked perfect from the outside, but there was darkness, bitterness, and resentfulness on the inside.

Then God began to make himself evident to us in the depth of our despair. During my internship we purchased a small home in a wonderful neighborhood in Durham. Across the street lived Walter and Gertrude Eakes, an older couple with unmarried adult boys. This sweet couple was praying that God would move a family with children across the street for whom they could be honorary grandparents. Next to our home were Margaret and Richard Scearce. They were empty nesters who loved counseling and mentoring younger couples. They were praying that God would move in a couple they could disciple. Next door to the Scearces was a house shared by four single Christian men who were Duke physicians. Three were psychiatry residents, and the fourth was a resident in internal medicine. They were praying that God would move in one psychologically and spiritually messed-up man they could minister to.

Catty-corner to our home was a small church with a new pastor. Several of the nurses who worshiped there worked at the Lenox Baker Children's Hospital, formerly the North Carolina Cerebral Palsy Hospital. They let their pastor know they felt the Lord was leading them to begin a respite ministry—a ministry for parents of children with disabilities.

Back then, 80 to 90 percent of parents of children with a disability got divorced. These wonderful ladies wanted to use the church on weekends to care for those children so the parents could have a break to care for themselves—to get some rest, respite, and reprieve from the daily work of caring for a child with a disability. The pastor told the nurses he loved the idea but wasn't aware of any children with a disability in the neighborhood. The ladies told him, "Not a problem. We'll pray that the Lord either moves someone in or shows us where they are."

We were the answer to *all* of their prayers! And God began to work. As these men and women loved my family and me by caring for, praying for, babysitting for, cooking for, and counseling us, God, ever so surely, began to pull us out of the mire in which we had been wallowing. God used that community of Christ followers to save me and save our marriage. I'm eternally grateful to him and them.

We slowly released our hopes and expectations that Kate would be a completely normal little girl. We accepted that she would not physically or mentally be like other girls; we acknowledged and understood we might need to serve and assist her for the rest of our lives. But we resolved to see her not as "disabled" but "differently abled" and determined to discover where she was exceptional.

Toward the end of our time in Durham, as our marriage and our love for each other was restored, we poured ourselves into Kate. We were taking her to endless sessions of therapy and reading, singing, and praying to her without stopping. What we didn't know was that her brain was being rewired in unique ways.

Our neighbors and friends joined in on the prayers. Kate became stronger, was able to sit and scoot around a little, and finally, with much assistance, was able to stand against a couch or chair. Her smile radiated across the room with each new accomplishment.

This precious and wonderful community was patient with us, helped us when we were at our weakest, and continually encouraged us. Through them, we learned that healing happens best in the context of a loving and supportive community.

I was seeing patients at the residency one afternoon when Barb called. "We're safe," she started, "but I need you to come home now! Will you?"

I could tell by her tone that this was *not* a question. My supervising physician was gracious enough to take my few remaining patients. I drove home as quickly as I could. When I rushed into the house, I found Kate sitting on the floor next to our couch, laughing and enjoying herself. She was thirty-six months old at the time.

Barb was seated near her, softly weeping. I hurried over and sat by her. "Honey, what's the matter? Are you okay?"

"Yes," Barb whispered between sobs. She reached over and took Kate's hand to help her stand up next to the couch. Then Barb scooted a few feet away. Kate stood there, smiling and laughing.

"Come on," Barb urged. "You can do it."

Very carefully, despite her muscular spasticity and limited joint motion, Kate leaned forward and slowly took a shaky step toward her mother, whose arms were outstretched.

"Come on, baby," Barb exclaimed. "You can do it!"

Kate took two more rickety, cautious, painstaking steps and fell into Barb's arms.

I couldn't believe my eyes! My little girl was walking! The doctors had said she never would or never could do that.

Barb held our daughter close as I leaned over to hug them both—Barb's and my tears mingling with Kate's shrieks of happiness.

"Walt," Bill said, breaking into my recollection, "Kate's a unique girl. Her mind is as sharp as a tack. She reads and talks and walks well, given her significant brain damage. Did she start talking when y'all moved to Bryson City?"

"That was an earlier miracle," I answered. "Against all the odds, she began talking in full sentences at about two and a half years of age. Dr. Reinuart, Kate's pediatric neurologist at Duke, said the constant prayers and therapy must have rewired her brain. Not only did her physical body change but she developed an amazing heart for God. Barb and I no longer concentrated on what she couldn't do but instead we focused on what she was designed and gifted to do. Not our plan for her life but God's plan. Today, Kate loves Jesus in a way Barb and I could only hope to."

Bill turned reflective. "So it sounds like your prayers for Kate were instantly heard and answered by God."

Instant? I thought, feeling confused. *It took years.* "How so?" I asked.

"God had a plan for her—just not the one *you* wanted or on *your* time line. But he *was* listening, as he always does. It's just rather than answering 'yes' right away, he took a little longer. It turned out he had something better for you, Barb, and Kate. My point is that God always hears our prayers. Sometimes he answers, 'yes,' at other times 'no,' and quite often, 'wait.'"

I nodded. "I've often wondered whether God partially healed Kate, or did he just design her to operate on fewer neurons than the rest of us? I don't know. Maybe one day, we'll repeat her CT scan and know more."

"I know this," John said. "Every child with a disability I have *ever* cared for has an amazing spiritual sensitivity. They see and hear angels that most folks don't. And they have a special relationship with God. From my way of thinking, that's the best healing of all."

John's comment caused me to remember a poem I had come across a month earlier. "Just a moment," I said, before stepping into the house, grabbing my Bible, and returning. I flipped through my Bible, then located and unfolded a piece of paper.

"Here it is," I said. "Claudia Minden Weisz wrote it a few years ago after many years of caring for her daughter who had a severe disability. I think it sums up what we've been talking about. And it has become my heart's prayer for myself, my marriage, my children, and my practice. She called it, 'And God Said, "No."'" I cleared my throat and read:

> I asked God to take away my pride, and God said, "No."
> He said it was not for him to take away, but for me to
>   give up.
> I asked God to grant me patience, and God said, "No."
> He said that patience is a by-product of tribulation; it's
>   not granted, it's earned.
> I asked God to give me happiness, and God said, "No."
> He said he gives me blessings; happiness is up to me.
> I asked God to spare me pain, and God said, "No."
> He said suffering draws me apart from worldly cares,
>   bringing me closer to him.
> I asked God to make my spirit grow, and God said, "No."
> He said I must grow on my own, but he will prune me to
>   make me fruitful.
> I asked God to make my disabled child whole, and God
>   said, "No."
> He said her spirit is whole; her body is only temporary.
> I asked God to help me love others as much as he loves me,
>   and God said,
> "Ah, finally you have the idea."[1]

We were quiet for a few moments, each lost in the inspiration of the beautiful poem. "God not only made Kate's spirit whole," I said softly, "but after two and a half years of living a horrible nightmare, Barb and I were finally back on the same team. Our faith grew stronger, and our marriage began to heal because a loving Father worked through each of the Christians he put into our lives. God began healing our daughter, me, and our marriage. I'm eternally grateful."

"Well," Bill said, "that's what I'd call a miraculous story. How about we just stop and thank the Lord right now for what he's done, what he's doing now, and what he will continue to do in each of our families?"

We bowed our heads, held hands, and listened to Bill pray for my family and me. I felt at home. Peaceful, comfortable, shielded, safe, and growing more rapidly spiritually than I ever had.

What happened at that barbecue was just the beginning of some additional beautiful lessons I was about to encounter.

20

Where Y'at?

WHILE ON MY MEDICAL SCHOOL PSYCHIATRY ROTATION at
Charity Hospital in New Orleans, one of the residents, a Cajun
man who had grown up in the swamps of South Louisiana, would
ask his patients, "Where y'at?" He wasn't inquiring about their
geographical location, but asking, "How are you doing? Where
are 'you at' today emotionally?"

To my surprise, the vast majority of folks knew exactly what
he meant.

"To help a patient take their next step for healing, you need to
know where they're at," he instructed us. "That includes where
they're coming from, where they are on their journey, and where
they want to go next. It's more important to find out from our
patients what matters than it is to ask, What's the matter? A good
physician treats the disease; a great physician treats the patient
who has the disease[1] for it's much more important to know what
sort of a patient a disease has, rather than what sort of disease
a patient has."[2]

Now that John and I were considering how to care for all of
our patients spiritually, we realized we would have to be aware of

where they were on their spiritual journey—or if they even wanted spiritual care. For example, it would be unwise to write a faith prescription to a depressed patient, listing Bible verses that speak about hope or recovery from depression, if they have no respect or even disdain for the Bible. Doing so could cause an emotional, "allergic," or hostile reaction.

Also, at times, a person's spiritual beliefs could change my medical care. I would never want to take a patient to surgery where bleeding was a significant risk and not know if the patient was a Jehovah's Witness. Why? Because people of that faith tradition often refuse blood transfusions based upon their sincerely held religious beliefs. When it comes to spiritual beliefs, physicians need to know where their patients "are at."

This meant we needed to learn how to take a spiritual history as part of our patient's social history—where we would ask about such things as substance abuse, occupation, hobbies and interests, travel, as well as exercise and diet preferences. The problem was, John and I were never taught how to perform a religious or spiritual assessment, so we began a search to find a way to do so.

Most of the spiritual histories we discovered in medical literature were involved, and some were very long. I decided to have a long phone discussion with a friend who John and I trained with at Duke. His name was David Larson, MD, and he'd served at the National Institute of Mental Health before founding and directing the National Institute of Healthcare Research. Dave, a Christian psychiatrist, suggested several examples of clinically useful approaches to collecting spiritual histories. Each consisted of three to five questions. He encouraged us to use these questions as a basis to develop our own.

After he sent the lists of questions, we picked and adapted three that I called "The GOD Questions."

The G of the GOD acrostic stood for *God*. We'd start by asking, "Do you have a spiritual, religious, or faith preference?" or "Are

God, faith, prayer, religion, or spirituality important to you?" If the patient said "yes," we'd explore how so.

The O stood for *Others*. We'd inquire, "Are you now or have you ever been part of a faith or spiritual community?" Again, if they answered in the positive, we'd ask how important and supportive that community was for them and how we might incorporate their community, if appropriate, in their care.

Last, the D stood for *Do*. We might ask, "Do you have any particular religious or spiritual beliefs we need to be aware of as we care for you?" or "Do you need any spiritual resources?" or "Do you want to see a pastoral professional or chaplain?" or "Would you mind if I prayed for you?" Of course, the specific questions would change from patient to patient, depending upon their responses and needs.

I mentioned my initial discomfort about adding several spiritual questions to our social history to Bill. When he asked why, I explained it was because patients might see these questions as odd or out of place in a medical interview.

"Well, I don't think you need to worry about that," Bill said.

"Why not?"

"Because your patients trust you and have confidence you know what you're doing. Besides, you physicians ask lots of strange questions all the time anyway."

I felt myself getting defensive. "Like what?!"

Bill thought a moment. "Not too long ago, I came in for my annual physical exam, and your nurse asked me how many sexual partners I'd had in the last year. That's a strange question to ask a man who has been married for over forty years, but I trusted she had a reason for asking. She must have noticed my quizzical look, and she explained why she asked—that having over one sexual partner could cause physical and emotional issues that might need addressing. That made sense to me, but I decided to kid around with her a bit.

"I furrowed my brow and said, 'So, how many sexual partners

have I had in the last twelve months? Well, I'm not sure.' Her eyes widened, and she gave me a puzzled look. Then I said, 'I'm not sure if the answer is zero or one.' It took her a second to realize that I was just joshing her. We both had a good chuckle about that!"

One of the first patients with whom I took a spiritual history was Leon. He was a small, older man who often came to the practice with his wife, who was even more medically frail and fragile than he. When I asked the G question, he looked incredulous and gave me a colorfully expressed "no!" With some apprehension, I asked the O question, and in no uncertain terms, he exclaimed even more colorfully, "No!" I was so surprised by his responses that I forgot to ask any D questions. But it gave me a clue that he must have had significant issues with some religious system or people to have such a negative response. I knew I'd have to explore that with him in the future.

Later Leon developed cancer, and as is common with patients who suddenly confront their mortality, he began thinking spiritual thoughts and opened up to me about them. It turns out that just trying to find out "where he was at" with his spiritual history let him know that I was at least willing to discuss spiritual issues.

We had many meaningful conversations, initially at the office and later during visits away from the practice. How far did he get with the many ministeps of his faith journey? I'll come back to that in a bit because I first want you to meet Gail.

Gail was a patient John prayed with at every visit. He recorded her answers to the GOD questions on her chart. By G and O, it said, "None." Unfortunately, I had not read further, as by D it said, "Prayer desired every visit."

Had I noticed that, I would have known "where she was at" spiritually and it would have been far less embarrassing when I saw her for a quick visit to refill some of her medications. As I was wrapping up our time, she said, "Are you done?"

I felt my brow furrow. "I think so. Is there something else?"

She gazed at me with a surprised look. This was a stern woman, rather uncultured in dress, demeanor, and dialect. "Salty," I think was the way John referred to her.

"Dr. John *always* ends our visit with prayer." She looked at me, waiting for a response. Perhaps seeing my surprise, she repeated "always," as she bowed her head.

I don't remember what I prayed, but afterward, she smiled, patted my arm, and said, "Not bad, Doc!"

I appreciated her humor, but our conversation was an excellent lesson for me—especially when Gail later came to know and trust the Lord. She attributed it to John's and my prayers *for* her and *with* her. That all happened, of course, because we took the time to find out "where she was at." She once told me, "When you and Dr. John would pray for me, I felt you were inviting the King of the Universe into my world, into the midst of my problems."

Toward the end of her life, she became one of our practice's most faithful prayer warriors. Every day we'd send her a list of prayer requests, and if we forgot, she'd call before we closed to get them. She would often say, "I'm not an educated woman, and I know my prayers are unschooled and probably don't sound very religious, but I believe they are profitable and powerful for two reasons. First, it's because they are persistent. But more importantly, the impact of my prayers doesn't depend upon my wording but on the one who hears them!"

I loved her down-home wisdom. Another time, Gail told me, "You tell your patients who are struggling with the storms of life, 'If trials give you more than you can stand, then you need to kneel!'" She would remind me, "I can't explain the power of prayer, but I love experiencing it in my life and the lives of our patients."

I loved that she said *our* patients, and I took no offense. Gail became a critical part of our spiritual care team and in the spiritual journeys of so many of our patients—passages we learned about by merely inquiring, "Where y'at?"

I've found that's a good question for physicians to ask every patient, but especially for difficult patients like Margie, whom I think you'll enjoy meeting next.

21

Margie

MARGIE WAS, IN A WORD, HYPOCHONDRIACAL. She mani-
fested a functional disorder in which her anxiety, obsessive-
compulsiveness, and myriad physical complaints, without *any*
objective evidence of disease, dominated her personality, thoughts,
and actions. Now, she did have some *real* medical issues—but
most were not. As a result, I could expect to see her once or twice
a month with a long rotating list of complaints.

Her primary physician was a well-known internist in Orlando,
but like most hypochondriacs, she saw more than one doctor since
no one could "fix" her. I think she chose me because our office
was closer to her home and it was more convenient for her to
complain to me.

Patients like Margie can try the patience of any family physician
because they choose, either consciously or unconsciously, never to
get well. They seem loath to ever admit it, however.

Unsuspecting or inexperienced physicians can be duped into
spending countless dollars for endless tests that invariably turn
out to be normal. Hypochondriacal people not only make themselves and their doctors miserable, but they cost society billions

of dollars in wasted health-care spending and lost productivity. The best treatments involve reassurance, reduction of anxiety, and preventing the temptation of the hypochondriac to doctor-hop. Spiritual interventions can also be beneficial should the patient be open to them.

I had taken a spiritual inventory during one of Margie's first visits to the office. I asked her the first question, the G question: "Is God, spirituality, or religion of any importance to you?"

"Nope," was her curt reply.

I pressed on with the O question: "Do you ever meet with others in a faith community? Do you ever attend church or synagogue?"

"Nooooooo way!" was the shrill retort. "Never have and never will!"

Just like with Leon, I was fearful to ask the D question, but for the sake of completeness, I pressed on. "Margie, is there anything I can do to help you in your spiritual journey?"

"Are you nuts?!" was all she could squeeze out between her pursed lips.

Oh well, I thought. *At least I know where y'at spiritually.* Not only was Margie not open to any direct spiritual interventions, but it also would not have surprised me if she *opposed* them.

But one intervention I could utilize without consent was to pray for her and have Gail pray for her. I kept a framed quote at my dictation station that Gail had given me as a gift. It was from pastor and theologian J. Sidlow Baxter and said this: "People may spurn our appeals, reject our message, oppose our arguments, and despise our persons, but they are helpless against our prayers."[1]

Despite our distinct differences spiritually, Margie continued to call me her family physician and began to show me a side of her I had never seen in previous visits.

"I'm tired of driving to Orlando to see the internist," Margie told me one day. "I'm afraid he will not be around much longer."

"Why's that?" I asked.

She giggled, putting her hand over her mouth, blushing. "Oh, honey, I don't think he knows how to live very well. He smokes and drinks and chews and runs around with girls who do." She broke out in a deep chortle, adding, "I'll tell him jokes, but he *never* laughs."

"Well, you've never told *me* any jokes."

She scowled. "It's because I don't like you as much as him. Anyway, I told him one time that I saw a gastroenterologist because I would get severe heartburn every time I ate birthday cake. The GI doctor's advice was that the next time I was at a birthday party, I should blow out the candles first." She chuckled, and I couldn't help but smile.

"Another time," she said, "I told him I had accidentally swallowed two coins. When he asked me how I was doing, I told him there was no change yet!" She howled, and I laughed with her.

At our next visit, Margie began by handing me an obituary she had cut from the paper. She explained that it was her former internist. "Guess you're stuck with me now!" she said, chuckling.

Even though I smiled, I groaned inside.

One afternoon I noticed Judy doubled over in laughter as Margie left the office. I had prescribed medication to help Margie with occasional insomnia, but she also was taking a laxative for bouts of constipation. She had said to Judy, "Honey, whatever else you do, never, never, under any circumstances, have a patient take a sleeping pill and a laxative on the same night."

As our doctor-patient relationship strengthened, I was slowly able to bring her physical and emotional disorders under control. One day, at the end of our visit, I felt led to run a faith flag up the pole. "Margie, you know what?"

"What?"

"I've been praying about you."

"Me?"

I nodded. "I've been thanking the Lord for the privilege he gives me to care for you and that you're finally working on getting a little better."

Her eyes narrowed. "A little better?"

"I know you don't believe in God or prayer, but I believe he's real, and talking to him is effective. And in your case, I think he's answering."

She responded with a *harrumph*!

I took a deep breath and decided to be a bit bolder. "Since I've come to know God personally, he's changed me, my marriage, and my family. I'm praying you'll come to know him and his love for you one day. I really am."

Her eyes widened, and her face turned red. I was expecting to be blasted when those widened eyes misted, and she reached out to touch my arm. "Doc, I can't tell you how much I appreciate that. I do. But I'm not so sure it will do any good." I handed her a Kleenex, and she wiped her eyes. "I just hope he hears you."

I smiled. "He does, Margie. I know that for a fact."

There's more to Margie's story, but first, I have to bring back Leon, the diminutive elderly man and his stirring story.

22

Leon

LEON RECOVERED FROM HIS CANCER, which is always miraculous for any patient, but especially for someone as old as him. I
watched his health improve a bit until his wife of fifty years passed
away suddenly. She wasn't only his soul mate, she was his only com-
panion. They had moved to Florida to escape the frigid winters of
their northern hometown, and although they found a warm (even
hot) environment in the Sunshine State, they had lost all of their
family and social support.

Leon's life had become absorbed in caring for his frail wife.
They had no acquaintances and never socialized with others. As
her condition worsened, so did his. I'd make frequent home visits
to see them, and in the back of my mind, I wondered who would
succumb first. If she preceded him, I was sure he'd die of a broken
heart. He was not open to my suggestion that he leave the house
for temporary breaks. As his strength and hope dwindled, his
wife's hospice nurses also had to care for him.

At her funeral, I witnessed a shattered man. Leon's grief was
palpable and heartbreaking. As I continued to visit him from time
to time at his home, I observed that his health was deteriorating.

He was so lonely, and his sadness deepened daily. He had outlived his parents, spouse, children, and extended family. I was sure he was dying not from illness but lonesomeness, and I explained to Judy that I expected him to graduate to glory any day.

As Barb and I had begun our journey of learning to weather the storms of life, we realized that God designed us for community—to thrive within healthy relationships and families. It's no surprise problems can result from being alone. In the first book of the Bible, Genesis, we are informed, "The LORD God formed a man from the dust of the ground and breathed into his nostrils the breath of life, and the man became a living being."[1] Several verses later, it says, "It is not good for the man to be alone."[2]

Being alone is a form of being incomplete—unable to be whole. The divine design is that chronic aloneness, for the most part, is the opposite of authentic living. Real life is not individual; it's social. It's living in community with others. Medical studies reveal that loneliness can cause psychiatric disorders, mental breakdowns, and even physical illness and premature death. For most folks, genuine living involves sharing life and love with others while loving and serving God, family, friends, and their community.

I wanted this to happen to Leon—to find something, anything, to rekindle his fire, recharge his batteries, rejuvenate his health, and reactivate his will to live. Something to turn him on and turn him around physically, emotionally, relationally, and spiritually. I had almost given up. His house and his soul were so depressing, dismal, and dark. His gloom was suffocating what spark remained in his heart and soul. I wanted to bring some brightness and lightness into his life, but I didn't see how I could do that.

One Saturday morning, while Barb and I shared coffee, she had a brilliant suggestion. "I noticed out in the greenhouse that one of the orchids has a gorgeous spray of spectacular, fragrant blooms. Why don't you take that orchid to Leon—to provide some color for him and his house."

As I walked out to our small greenhouse, I found a tiny kitten just outside. None of our neighbors knew where she came from or admitted placing her there. Wondering if a bobcat or gator had snatched her mother—not a rare occurrence in our neighborhood of lakeside homes—Barb suggested I give the kitty and the blooming flower to Leon.

"Perhaps these symbols of fresh life will give him a new lease on living," she said.

I drove to Makinson's Hardware Store and picked up supplies for caring for both the orchid and the kitten before heading to Leon's. I wasn't sure what his response would be, but as he received my gifts, a smile began to creep across his face—then it exploded ear to ear. It was the first grin I'd seen on him in quite some time—but not the last.

The kitten made him an instant celebrity in his trailer park. He later nicknamed the kitty Babe Magnet, referring to the widows who just happened to "drop by" to see how Leon and his little kitty were doing.

The orchid ignited his curiosity and creativity. He began visiting Jimmy and Cynthia Sabetto's orchid business, Tropic 1 Orchids, with me on Saturday mornings. He took classes from Jimmy in orchid care. His circle of friends grew, as did his confidence to live life to the fullest.

As his "Babe Magnet" grew, so did Leon's vigor and vivaciousness. He seemed to bloom in fresh ways with each new orchid he purchased. He loved bringing them to the office when they flowered to show them off to my staff and me. The female staff members would croon over him and his blooms.

He loved the attention, and then he surprised us all.

23

Patients and Friends

ONE MORNING, when I walked into the exam room, Margie exploded from her chair with a hearty laugh and hurried across the room to hug me. She had *never* done that before.

"Margie!" I exclaimed. "What are you so happy about? You seem almost giddy. Have you been drinking again?" I kidded her.

"Not before noon!" she joshed back. And then turning serious, she added, "Doc, you'll never believe it, but the Lord has *finally* answered your prayers!"

"What in the world are you talking about?"

"I've begun going to church. Not 'cause I wanted to, mind you, but because my neighbor wouldn't stop pestering me. I first went just to be neighborly and try to get him off my back, but then, you know what? I actually enjoyed church. And believe it or not, I've learned some things about myself. I'm not saying I ever liked the way I was, but I knew no other way."

"What did you like about going to church?" I figured her answer would tell me a lot about where she "was at."

"The pastor made sense to me. He began to encourage me to

pray and read the Bible. I don't know what happened, but something did happen, and now I'm not the same woman!"

She looked me straight in the eyes. "Doc, thanks for praying for me and caring for me—but most of all, thanks for caring *about* me."

Before I could respond, she added, "Oh, and you should know something else. The good news is that I'm seeing someone. The bad news is that he's living with another woman."

"What?" This wasn't going in the right direction.

"Don't seem so surprised. After all, you know him. He's one of your favorite patients. After me, that is."

"Do tell. You can dish."

She smiled and blushed as she said, "It's Leon and his girlfriend, Babe."

Margie's and Leon's spiritual transformations were spectacular, which resulted in improvements in their emotional, relational, and physical health, although Margie's innate curtness never disappeared, which I kind of liked.

Every time I saw her and asked how she was doing, she would quote her favorite verse, which was possible because she was beginning to memorize Scripture. The one she shared with me was this: "Anyone who belongs to Christ has become a new person. The old life is gone; a new life has begun!"[1]

One day she added, "How many gals do you know, Doc, who are reborn when they're as old as me? And, you've got to admit, I'm a pretty hot-looking 'new creature' for my age!"

While the Bible promises no one a perfectly healthy physical life, it promises those who have a vibrant personal relationship with God that they will experience an abundant life: a life that will be full and meaningful, infused with purpose, contentment, and joy.[2] Leon and Margie were dramatic recipients of those very promises but not unique. Of the hundreds of spiritual-healing cases I observed through the decades, most experienced significant improvements in their emotional and relational health along with a dramatic improvement in their ability to cope with their illnesses.

As we continued to work on Margie's several physical and emotional ailments, she would tell me, "Minor mechanical problems aren't too noticeable in older vehicles that are otherwise running efficiently."

She had a point: Margie was running efficiently and proficiently. She always had a smile and a kind word for me and everyone on our staff.

It was no surprise to me that, against all medical odds, Leon and Margie lived for another ten years. During that time, they lived full and complete lives. For me, they became living proof that the value of spiritual birth combined with meaningful relationships, interests, hobbies, and pets not only nurtures excellent health but also restores declining and downward-spiraling life.

Without these things I believe I would have attended their funerals many years earlier—and with much less joy. But at their memorial services, I knew they had both graduated to glory, and there was nothing better than that.

Leon died first, and at his funeral, his pastor reminded us, "Death is not the extinguishing of a light after which darkness descends. No! Not even close! Rather, it is quenching the lamp of a Christian because the dawn has come, and the Son is rising. For our friend Leon, his body is still here, but he is not. He is already with the Lord. Even though Jesus healed hundreds and fed thousands, he only raised three from the dead. Why so few? I believe it's because after tasting heaven, few would volunteer to come back. Compared to paradise, this valley of storms and tears is the *last* place most people would want to return to! So don't cry for Leon because he's not complaining. He's gloriously happy in glory. Or, as I often tell my congregation, 'hope for tomorrow makes up for a lot of yesterday's disappointments.'"

I'll never forget my last interaction in the office with Margie. We were walking toward the checkout counter and talking about aging.

"Doc," she said, "are you aware of the three sure signs of old age?" She had a devilish smirk on her face and a gleam in her eye. *Here comes another joke*, I thought, so I played along.

"No, Margie, I am not. What are they?"

"Well, the first is that you lose your memory, and the second is . . . uh . . ."

I laughed, realizing she had just yanked my chain again. She joined me in laughing, not only as my oldest patient but also as a dear friend and a spiritual sister.

When Margie died, she did so peacefully. When I pronounced her, her facial expression appeared to be a smile. At the funeral, her daughter handed me a card. Inside, it said:

Doc, be sure that the kids have this engraved on the back of my tombstone. "See, I told you I was sick." Not really. I'd prefer you have the kids engrave my chocolate chip cookie recipe. It's hidden on a note card in my kitchen recipe box. Every time you and your staff asked for the recipe, I told you, "Over my dead body!" Now it will be!

Seriously, when you first diagnosed me as a hypochondriac, I remember thinking, "But, Doc, I'd like a fifteenth opinion." Once, I told you, "Will you please stop calling me a hypochondriac? I'm sick of it." Then you told me the most common symptoms of being hypochondriacal, and I had them all. You'd make up the name of a fake illness just to see how long it took me to come down with it.

Well, I guess I'm not being serious at all, am I? So I will be for once. Thanks for loving Leon and me. Thanks for praying for and with us. Thanks for caring for and about us.

I love you.

Margie

I loved having patients like Margie and Leon, who became dear friends. I adored patients like them because they also became my spiritual brother and sister. Leon and Margie were like that, and they sure lived their final season that way.

I'm happy they were my patients *and* my friends.

24

Amazing Bull

ON THE LAST DAY OF ANOTHER SILVER SPURS RODEO, nearly eight thousand folks packed the grandstand on a humid Sunday afternoon. The sounds of the adjacent county fair midway wafted across the arena, combining with the pungent smells from the stockyard. Musty, earthy odors rose off the freshly tilled arena soil, and the delicious scents of barbecued hamburgers and buttery popcorn drifted through the still, muggy air. I was wrapped in a comfortable quilt of unforgettable sensations.

My preteen son, Scott, and his same-aged friend, Scott Ramsey, Alice's son, sat on top of the protective steel fencing that encircled the arena. The fencing had been made from eight-foot-long, two-inch in diameter, horizontal steel bars, that were welded every eight inches to vertical steel supports and bolted into ten-by-ten-inch vertical timbers. I remember thinking a Sherman tank would not be able to knock down that fencing.

As always, Alice and I sat in our usual chairs by the arena barrier outside the First-Aid room. Geech was happy to sit on his electric scooter and take everything in. After the opening ceremonies that included Clem, our world-famous rodeo announcer, offering his traditional cowboy prayer, the competition always began and ended with bull riding. Geech always said it was marketing genius.

"Bull riding's what most folks are coming to watch. Give 'em a bit to wet their whistles, and they'll sure as shootin' stay until the end. The concession stands will do a ton of business, and the Spurs will make even more money to donate to local charities."

"Which ones do you all support?" I asked.

"Each rodeo, the Silver Spurs Club selects a local nonprofit or organization as the beneficiary. In the past, we've donated to the Center for Children and Families, the Guardian ad Litem Foundation, Give Kids the World, Horses for Heroes, Habitat for Humanity, and others. But that's not all. Every year we host free community events, like the Special Rodeo, which gives children with disabilities the opportunity to experience rodeo. I'm proud to be a part of 'em."

Alice chuckled. "He's more than part of them. He's one of our founding members."

After watching the first man get thrown off and observing in amazement the speed and skill of the bullfighters in distracting the bull from the rider, the entire crowd was enthralled and captivated. As the event went on, a couple of the bull riders and even the bullfighters were also hooked—but in their cases, by the bull's dangerous horns. Observing the power of these 1,500-to-2,000-pound beasts up close was awe-inspiring.

"Are there any bulls that just can't be ridden?" I asked Geech.

"Simple answer, son. There never was a bull that couldn't be rode, and there never was a cowboy couldn't be throwed."

"Has there ever been a perfect ride?"

"Just one—and not too long ago. Up at the Wild Rogue Rodeo in Oregon. A little tiny fellow by the name of Wade Leslie—stood just over five feet tall and weighed about 125 pounds soakin' wet. They say he was a horseshoer from Moses Lake. He drew a nasty 2,000-pound bull named Wolfman Skoal. The two PRCA judges, both of 'em expert judges—I know 'em both—gave the cowboy *and* the bull a perfect score. The first and only 100-point ride in PRCA history. I'd liked to have seen that ride! I know that bull, and he's rank—been to the National Finals Rodeo four times and voted as the Bucking Bull of the Year once. Makes him one dangerous beast, that's for darn sure."[1]

Sitting beside the arena gave me a deep appreciation of the sport—both the creatures and their human competitors. But I never truly understood how truly dangerous a bull can be until I was nearly severely injured by one firsthand.

After an 1,800-pound bull named Nasty Ned, a National Finals Rodeo bull, tossed an experienced cowboy in two to three seconds by spinning like a helicopter, he rotated to a halt about fifteen feet from our fence and faced us. He lowered his massive head, snorted, and pawed the dirt. Geech, who was sitting by me in his scooter, threw it in reverse and quickly backed up. I remember turning my head toward him, snickering to myself, and thinking, *Geech has gotten too old. I can't believe he's backing up. We're perfectly safe here!*

In a single instant, I heard Scott Ramsey shriek to my son, "Scott, jump! Now!"

Both boys leaped safely to the ground next to me. That's when Alice screamed from behind. "Doc, back up!"

At the same second, I saw a blur out of the corner of my eye. I froze—too shocked to move. The bull hurtled straight for me, and its head struck the gate at full speed, just inches from my head. The two-inch steel rods were barely a match for the brute and bent in several inches. I had never been so petrified in my life. The bull's mucous sprayed over me as the ground shook. His sweat pelted me like I was being sandblasted, and his rank stench washed over me like a wave.

I was helpless; every muscle fiber was frozen in horror. Before I could move or gasp or think or react, two bullfighters swatted the bull's snout, and he spun and sprinted away to take his considerable fury out on them.

Geech scooted up again. "Sorry about that, Doc. I knew he was comin' at us. I saw it in his eyes and didn't have time to yell at 'cha."

Alice came up beside me and handed me a towel. "Wow! That was a close one, Dr. Larimore."

I took a deep breath as I wiped my face, neck, and the front of my shirt. My heart felt like it would pound out of my chest; a cold sweat drenched my brow. I tried to speak, but no words escaped my cotton-dry mouth. I looked around. Both boys were safe, laughing and slapping each other on the back.

Geech chuckled. "Well, we're lucky that sucker didn't jump the fence."

I looked at him like he was crazy. "That's a two-ton bull. The fence is at least seven feet tall."

"Not a problem for most of 'em. They're agile animals. Not at all unusual to see 'em clear six-to-eight-foot fences if they get a mind to—both at rodeos and in the fields. I always say, 'If you get to thinkin' you're a person of some influence or power, try orderin' a rodeo bull around!'"

"Well, it's a good lesson for me," I whispered.

"I've found that the old saying is true: 'Good judgment comes from experience, and experience . . . well, that comes from poor judgment,'" Geech crooned. "My daddy always said, 'Experience is the name everyone gives to their mistakes.'"[2]

I nodded and clasped my hands together—both to hide the trembling and to express a quick prayer of thanks.

"Oh, and one more thing," Geech added. "Never approach a bull from the front, a horse from the rear, or a fool from any direction."

After Nasty Ned was wrangled back into the holding pen, the bull riding continued until the last bull of the competition exploded out of the chute, bucking and spinning like a maniac. How the rider stayed on was beyond me. The crowd rose to its feet, cheering him on. The bull landed on his hind legs, and one bent at a terrible angle. To my astonishment, the beast collapsed and didn't move. The rider had a leg pinned underneath the bull but appeared to be okay.

"That bull has a broke leg!" Geech bellowed. "That's what it is. When a 2,000-pound bull leaps five or six feet up in the air and sledgehammers on his back legs into the ground, it can be bad—a broke bone, snapped ligament or tendon, or a blown-out joint. It's surprising it's as rare as it is. But watch this! They train the boys for this."

The bullfighters jumped into action. One helped the rider extricate his trapped leg from under the bull while the other one ripped off one of the several colorful bandanas from his belt, jumped on the bull's neck, and wrapped it around the bull's eyes.

"The bull knows he's hurt bad," Geech explained. "That's why he went to the ground. Blinding him will keep him calm."

As a man ran across the arena, Geech continued his running commentary.

"That there's my friend Pete Clemons. He provides a lot of our stock and owns the Okeechobee Livestock Market. Like my folks, his parents came from pioneer Florida cattle families. Pete was a pro rodeo performer from high school well into his forties. In fact, he holds a record that still stands—eight All-Around titles here at the Silver Spurs Rodeo. To win that All-Around saddle, you gotta excel in five events: saddle bronc, bareback bronc, calf roping, steer wrestling, *and* bull riding. He could do it all. In fact, Pete was the model for the Kowboy Jake cartoon character that's been the honorary mascot for the Osceola High School Kowboy athletic teams since before 1950."

In the arena, Pete stood and motioned to the chutes. "I bet he's calling the vet," Geech explained.

A skinny man sprinted across the field toward the bull. As he knelt by its head, I saw a syringe in his hand but suspected most of the spectators could not. He inserted the needle into the large jugular vein in the bull's neck, injected, and in only a second or two, the bull relaxed and was out of its misery.

Clem explained the circumstances to the crowd. "Ladies and gentlemen, you've seen the care and respect given these mighty beasts by rodeo staff. One bullfighter first protected the cowboy, and another covered the bull's eyes to calm him down. Our rodeo vet was here, as you witnessed, in mere seconds, and administered a powerful sedative into the bull's massive jugular vein, and he was instantly pain-free. He was humanely put down, and he will be respectfully laid to rest at the edge of his home pasture."

The bullfighters, the rider, and the vet waited as several competitors leaped over the fence, ran toward, and then stood around the animal. "The cowboys are showing their respect for this bull," Clem told the crowd. "They know rodeo requires a working relationship, a partnership between the cowboy and the stock. Both are athletes in their own right. Cowboys and stockmen value their animals and are maybe some of the most pro-animal folks you'll ever meet. They believe all stock should be provided proper respect, care, and treatment."

A Dodge Ram pickup truck, a favorite vehicle of the cowboys, drove into the arena. They attached a rope from the trailer hitch to the bull's horns and pulled the beast from the ring as the men all followed.

Geech noted, "The men'll accompany the bull out of the ring as a way of showing their respect. I can tell you this about Pete: his stock becomes respected and valued members of his family. Pete'll load him up and take him back to his ranch, where he'll have a respectful burial. Wouldn't be surprised if'n he didn't shed a tear or two."

I looked at Geech. His eyes misted. It was a somber end to that year's rodeo, which was, as usual, where I always learned a bit more about my hometown and her pioneers.

However, I still had another lesson to learn that evening.[3]

25

Memorable Auctions

THAT EVENING, AFTER THE RODEO, Scott and I walked over
to the Osceola County Fair and Kissimmee Valley Livestock Show,
which had been an annual event for over forty years. The livestock
show was held next to and concurrent with the rodeo.

As we enjoyed a few of the seventy rides and games on the
midway, we feasted—or some might say gorged—on some not-
so-healthy but tasty funnel cakes, cotton candy, and waffle cones.
From our amazement at the truck and tractor pull to our laughter
at a pie-eating contest, we reveled in the nostalgia of Americana
at its best.

While crews set up the rodeo stadium for that night's country
music concert, we toured the 4-H exhibits and various competi-
tions, including baked goods, crafts, and a remarkable menag-
erie of farm animals. Bill Judge was our tour guide and told us
that most of the volunteers and exhibitors were third-to-fifth-
generation Osceoleans. Their families were founding members
of our county and the 4-H organization.

Bill sold calves to the young 4-H'ers, which they then raised

for auction. Bill was there to help us buy a steer. He encouraged John and me to join the annual festivities since a purchase
would be excellent PR for our practice, allow us to support a
local youngster, and provide an economical supply of organic
protein for our families. We decided to, as they say, throw our
hats into the ring.

County Commissioner Randy Sheive, who owned a meat-
packing plant, would take the steers purchased, humanely butcher
them, then wrap and freeze the various cuts of beef and schedule
delivery to your home once a quarter. In our case, John and I would
split the cost and product.

John was at the hospital, caring for patients, so it was up to
Scott and me to purchase under Bill's expert supervision. We
walked the paddock with Bill, examining each animal and making mental notes.

At the registration table, Bill introduced us to auctioneer Don
Shearer. "Don does most of the charity auctions around here. In
fact, he's Disney World's top auctioneer when they need one. And
he serves our county as a deputy sheriff."

Don blushed. "Best of all, Doc, I'm daddy to Donnita and Jennifer. That's my most important job."

I immediately liked the man, but he stirred a memory. "I think
we met at the First Baptist Church," I said. "Barb and I were visiting on Tim Wilder's first day."

Don broke out in a belly laugh. "That spiritual gift of ventrilo-
quism was one of the funniest things I've ever seen. Gosh, I love
that guy!" He gave me a once-over. "And I was in charge of the
safety crew when you burned down your house."

Bill put a friendly arm around Don's shoulder. "But his greatest gift, besides all the community service he does, is these charity
auctions."

Don leaned toward me and whispered, "My wife, Janet, says
I'm addicted to auctions, but she's wrong. I actually stopped after
going once . . . going twice . . . and gone . . ."

We all laughed.

"Well, y'all bid high," Don said. "It's all for a good cause. Now, if you'll excuse me, I need to go greet some of these rich . . . I mean, good folks."

After finishing registration as buyers and receiving our bidding paddle, we walked into the show barn, finding it packed with a standing-room-only crowd. Luckily Bill had reserved seats.

The first steer up for auction was the Grand Champion, who weighed in at over 1,200 pounds. Bill informed us that the grocery stores Winn-Dixie and Publix would always purchase the first two steers, the Grand and Reserve Champions, for very high prices. As the bidding continued, the winning prices could be expected to drop. "That means the value of these subsequent steers could actually be much better," Bill said.

After watching Don and his assistants lead the crowd through the auction of a couple dozen steers, he introduced a young lady who walked her massive steer into the show barn.

Bill chuckled. "He's got her outweighed by almost a ton and a half, yet she leads him like he's a small pet. That's the affection these animals have for the kids who feed and brush and walk them several times a day for months. It's a labor of love, and the kids have mixed feelings about selling them. They're attached to 'em." His eyes squinted, and he nodded. "Scott, we should go for this one."

As the auction progressed, Bill would suggest to Scott when to hold up his auction paddle. "Don't want to seem too anxious, Scott," he cautioned. "Don's president of the Florida Auctioneers Association and one of the best in the business. He's an expert at knowing how to push a bidder's emotional buttons."

Bill looked around at the audience. "Add to that the fact that this barn is full of people who are trying to see and be seen—to impress themselves and each other. So, my point is folks can get swept up—just like anybody might—at the moment's thrill. Adrenaline rushes and selfish emotions can block a person's ability to judge rationally, and they end up bidding more than they ever wanted to or should have. We need not encourage any unnecessary competition. We are just aiming for a good steer at a fair value for you and the 4-H student."

On this particular bull, Bill let the price increase. As potential buyers dropped out, he strategically had Scott raise our paddle whenever he wanted to up the bid—often waiting quite a few seconds after the previous bid before doing so. Whether it was his psychology or the immense respect so many folks in the room had for Bill, Don didn't push the crowd to bid against us. Before we knew it, Scott made the top bid for what Bill called a fantastic price.

During the polite applause, we all stepped into the ring. Don stepped off the stand for the requisite photograph of every auction winner. That's when he leaned over and whispered to Scott, "Son, you got ripped off."

"I did?" Scott asked.

"You got a Milk Dud." He laughed at his joke, but Scott didn't get it.

Don turned serious. "You need to buy a bell to put around that steer's neck."

"Why?" my son asked.

Don started to chuckle. "Because his horns don't work."

We were all still laughing when the photographer snapped our picture and as we walked to the stalls. The young lady, whose bull we'd bought, showed Scott how to brush the steer as I signed paperwork with Randy Sheive and completed the details of the order.

It had been an exhilarating day for my son and me—one we would never, ever forget. But the most memorable moment occurred on the way home. I was driving my old pickup truck down a pitch-dark county road. Scott and I were each in our thoughts when he said, "Dad, I want to name our steer LA."

"Why LA?"

"Because his hooves were so big that they remind me of big athletic shoes, like LA Gear."

I chuckled.

"Dad," Scott said, earnestly, "does Mom know about LA?"

"What do you mean?"

"I mean, we spent a lot of money. Does she know *that*?"

I appreciated the query because this allowed me to talk about having a budget and making financial decisions as a family. One of our rules was that we made no significant or "out-of-budget" purchases without the family's concurrence. His question told me he had tuned in to this teaching.

"We discussed it and budgeted for the purchase. You must not have been there that evening."

"Well," he added, matter-of-factly, "I'm sure I was not because I am very, very surprised!"

"Why?"

His next statement astonished me. I was entirely unprepared for it.

"Our backyard is so small, and LA will eat all of our lawn grass in one day!"

No wonder Scott had a name for the steer. He was sure we were purchasing a pet, not a food source.

I drew a deep breath. My mind was racing. What could I say to soften the coming blow? "Scott," I said, "we did not buy LA to be a pet."

All was quiet for a moment. "Do you mean you and Mom are gonna eat LA?" a small, quivering voice asked.

For the next six months, Scott became a vegetarian at our home. He would not eat hamburger or steak or even any bacon or pork chops, in solidarity with LA.

Over time, though, Scott's appetite for meat returned, and the pain of losing a pet lessened. Our son just needed some time to get there.

Don would always let Barb and me know when he was doing a charity auction. We started attending one of his larger local auctions each year. We had avoided it in the past, primarily because the event was too formal for us. Finally, Don agreed to lend me one of his tuxes—"I got more tuxes than an octopus has legs," he told me—so I conceded, and we showed up to one of the auctions.

The charity event was a glamorous, black-tie affair at a local Disney resort where Don was the AuctionEAR, a reference to the Mickey Mouse ears everyone wore. Every detail was first class, including the entertainment, food, and decorations. There were various magnificent and costly items available for both the silent and the live auctions.

During the silent auction, Barb and I munched on delicious hors d'oeuvres with Don and his wife while listening to the musicians softly playing music in the background. Don introduced us to the local politicos, Disney executives, and other movers and shakers.

One, Don pointed out, had the reputation of being an insufferably egotistical fellow. "He's a self-made man," Don whispered, "who worships his creator—that's with a little *c*." Don chuckled. "He's literally a legend in his own mind."

The man was quite handsome and appeared to be athletic, suave, and sophisticated—but Don was right. He reeked of pretentiousness and pride.

"Notice how he's working the crowd between jotting down his bids on the sheets for various items," Don pointed out. "I've noticed that a high-end leather briefcase has attracted his attention. No sooner than someone writes an offer than he'll slink up to the table and jot a higher bid on the line beneath theirs. He hates to lose, that's for sure!"

Don moved on to greet others, but my naughty side encouraged me to be one of those bidding against Mr. Ego, just to run up the price. Okay, I know this was not very kind or righteous, but it was kind of fun doing it anyway. I made sure he never saw me and only entered a bid when he turned away. Within minutes, he'd check the latest offer and raise his tender in ever-increasing amounts. As the purchase price approached three times the item's posted value, I worried that I could not afford the briefcase—which I found to be ugly and unattractive—if I somehow ended up being the final bidder. Even though that briefcase was the last thing I wanted, I wanted Mr. Ego to taste a slice of humble pie. So I topped his bid and waited for the man to return.

Sweat broke out on my forehead when Don Shearer began the countdown with only one minute left. Then with just seconds to go, Mr. Ego darted over, upped my bid, and stood proudly over his accomplishment. I released a sigh of relief—and realized I'd gotten lucky. I really shouldn't have bid up the price like that. This certainly wasn't a "What would Jesus do?" moment for me.

The magnificent meal and live auction raised tens of thousands of dollars for several worthy causes. As the festivities wound down, we said our goodbyes and were leaving the ballroom when I heard someone call out, "Dr. Larimore!" I turned to see Mr. Ego striding toward me with his prized briefcase in hand.

"What do you think of this beauty?" he asked gloatingly.

"It's fabulous!" I will admit that I was less than truthful, thinking that he must have seen me bidding against him. "Thanks for supporting such fantastic causes," I said.

He beamed, smiling from ear to ear. "Glad to hear you say that, Walt. With your and Dr. John's practice booming here in Kissimmee, I wanted to give you a gift to celebrate."

He handed the expensive briefcase to me. "Here, it's all yours. But if I ever find out who was bidding against me to drive up the price, I'll choke them!"

His generous gift astonished me. All I could do was mumble

my thanks as he wished me the best and turned to leave. I felt like a heel for my foolish actions of unnecessarily running up the bid just to spite Mr. Ego, but I remembered a cautionary proverb: "A fool repeats his foolishness."[1]

I hoped not to!

26

Seizure

When I arrived home from the office one evening, the house was empty, so I sat down to have a few quiet moments of reading the newspaper when the door from the garage flew open.

"Walt!" Barb cried. "Something's wrong with Kate!"

I leaped to my feet to see Barb half supporting and half carrying our eleven-year-old daughter, whose arm was draped over Barb's shoulder.

"Let's get her to her bedroom." I got under Kate's other arm. She appeared dazed as we hurried to lay her on the bed. I checked her pulse; it was racing.

"She was at Sam and Nancy Cunningham's house watching the movie *Heidi* when Nancy called to tell me something was wrong. Kate was complaining of dizziness, nausea, and blurred vision, and then her speech garbled. I picked her up, and on the way home, she got sick to her stomach and told me her arms and legs were too heavy to move. She kept calling me Klara. I drove home as fast as possible."

"Who is Klara?"

"A character in the movie—a girl with a disability."

"Daddy!" Kate cried. "I can't see."

I placed my hands on both cheeks and turned her head toward me. "Look at me, Kate."

Her voice raised a pitch, and she trembled as she slurred her words. "Daddy! I can't see! I can't hear you! My face and hands are numb!"

I thought she was panicking, so I gently slapped one cheek with my right hand. Her eyes rolled up, closed, and her entire body shook and convulsed. I felt like an utter fool—my daughter wasn't panicking, she was seizing!

"Walt, what's going on?" Barb cried.

I pulled Kate toward me and onto her side. "She's having a seizure, honey. She'll be fine. I'll protect her from hurting herself until it stops."

"Do I call 9-1-1? Or John?"

"Let's give her a moment. Most seizures last only a short time—two to three minutes at the most—and stop by themselves. Where's Scott?"

"He's spending the night at Cameron Madison's home."

Seconds seemed like hours. I was helpless to do anything but whisper a silent prayer as I stroked my daughter's forehead. Based upon her experience as a prenatal educator, Barb instinctively monitored her wristwatch and counted off each minute. With each pronouncement, though, Kate's convulsions continued, and my alarm levels increased. Had she fallen and struck her head? Did she have a bleed in her brain? *What's going on?* my mind silently screamed.

"Four minutes!" Barb exclaimed, the strain in her voice unmistakable. "Shall I call 9-1-1?"

I shook my head. "Call John. Tell him to meet us at the ER. I'll get Kate to the car."

Barb ran to the phone as I lifted Kate into my arms and hurried outside. Having a tonic-clonic seizure for five minutes or more is called *status epilepticus* and needs urgent treatment to stop it before it causes long-term harm. I knew if the seizure lasted for thirty minutes or longer, it could cause permanent brain damage or even death. We were five minutes into the seizure and less than five minutes from the hospital—but we'd still have to hurry!

I plopped down in the back seat, cradling Kate. Barb ran out to the car after completing her call, and I had her turn on the emergency blinkers as we headed to the ER. She was driving too fast, and I implored her, "Slow down, honey! Let's not get in a wreck. It'll only make things worse."

Kate did not stop seizing. Foam developed around her mouth, which I wiped off.

As Barb rolled through a stop sign and then floored it, I saw a Kissimmee police cruiser pull out and speed up beside us. Barb was in the left lane, and police officer Gib Michaels raced up by the passenger side. He must have recognized me and rolled down his window.

I yelled out, "Officer, Kate's having a seizure. Can you escort us to the ER?"

He nodded, rolled up his window, turned on his lights and siren, and speeded up to get in front of us.

As we screeched to a halt under the hospital emergency entrance, ER doctor Ken Byerly, nurse Sandi Lynch, and an orderly were at the door with a gurney. They whisked Kate inside. "Go park the car, Barb. Then go to the check-in desk. I'll come to you as soon as I can."

As she drove away, Gib ran up. He still had a slight limp, hardly noticeable at all, given the degree of the trauma he had sustained. "What happened, Doc?"

"Kate started seizing at home. I figured we could get her here to the ER faster than calling 9-1-1. I'm not sure that was the wisest decision."

"When Mrs. Larimore ran the stop sign and I saw you both, especially with you in the back and *not* in that ugly ole truck of yours, I knew something bad was going down." He reached up and put a hand on my shoulder. "I'm glad I could help. Now you go on in and make her better. You hear?"

I ran into the treatment room. Kate was on a heart monitor and Sandi had started an IV of normal saline and was labeling several tubes of blood she had drawn to check serum electrolytes, kidney function, glucose, a toxic drug screen, and a complete blood cell count. Another nurse placed Kate on oxygen and attached a pulse oximeter to her finger.

Dr. Byerly opened the crash cart. "Walt, her finger stick blood sugar is normal," he said, which was his way of telling me he had ruled out profound low blood sugar, or hypoglycemia, as a cause.

"Any history of trauma, poisoning, or epilepsy?" he asked. I could tell he was developing a differential diagnosis—thinking through reasons for her seizure—as he pulled out a vial and a syringe with a needle. After cleaning the stopper of the bottle with an alcohol swab, he plunged the needle in and drew up a medicine.

"Everything's been copasetic," I told him. "Kate has cerebral palsy, but she's never had a seizure. No heart, GI, or kidney issues. We all had strep throat and fever about two weeks ago. It went away after John gave us each a Rocephin shot. Last month she had her first menstrual period, but it was light and only lasted a few days."

"Blood pressure's normal!" Sandi called out. "She has no fever. Pulse and respiratory rates are coming down a bit. Oxygen level normal on two liters per minute. I've paged respiratory therapy stat to come draw a blood gas." That test, run on an arterial blood sample, would check Kate's oxygen levels and tell us if her acid level was abnormal.

"When did it start?" Ken asked.

I looked at my watch. "About fifteen to twenty minutes ago, although she had an aura for about thirty minutes before that."

An aura comprises the symptoms a person has right before a seizure. It's often an indescribable feeling, while other times, it may result in changes in perception, sensation, thought, or behavior. Other symptoms can be visual, auditory, or olfactory hallucinations, headache, dizziness or lightheadedness, nausea, or numbness or tingling in various parts of the body. In Kate's case, she experienced nausea, dizziness, blurred vision, and garbled speech.

Ken injected medication into Kate's IV line as she continued to seize. "I'm pushing ten milligrams of diazepam over two minutes."

I nodded. Diazepam, more commonly known as Valium, enters a patient's brain and ends a seizure of any type in at least 75 percent of those in status epilepticus. However, there were detrimental side effects, including respiratory suppression and hypotension, meaning profoundly low blood pressure. While we waited for the medicine to work, Ken examined Kate from head to toe. Watching him go over her as she continued to seize caused me to feel nauseous and weak.

An arm encircled my shoulders. "It's all right, Walt. I'm here."

It was John, dressed in his white lab coat.

"You don't look so good," he said. "Have a seat while I talk to Sandi and Ken."

Kate's seizure continued as I sat down and felt myself beginning to hyperventilate. John walked back to me and kneeled.

"She's still seizing. Ken will try a lorazepam injection." Lorazepam is another medicine in the same benzodiazepine class as diazepam and is used as a second drug if the first doesn't stop a seizure.

I tried to speak, but no words came, so I nodded.

"It's been thirty minutes, Walt. I need to put in a bladder catheter, a nasogastric tube, and intubate her. I can't risk her aspirating into her lungs."

"What if the lorazepam doesn't work?"

"The next step will be phenobarbital. I'm arranging an ICU bed and calling one of our neurologists to check on her. Anything else you can think of?"

I shook my head. My mind was racing but also caught in an

increasing fog. I shuddered, thinking my daughter would either become more brain-damaged or even die right in front of our eyes.

"How about we say a prayer?" John asked.

I nodded and then listened as John said a short, sweet prayer and hugged me. "I've got this. I want you to go out and sit with Barb. You care for her; I'll care for Kate. Sandi and I will keep you up-to-date."

I left the ER treatment room in a trance, numb from the events of the last hour, and feeling entirely helpless.

Right where God wanted me.

27

Death of a Dream

PASTOR PETE AND JUDY ZIEG walked into the ICU waiting room and greeted us. "Gib called to tell me about Kate," Pete said. "We came as quickly as we could. Chief Ross put out a notice to the police force and the other chaplains. Don Shearer is letting the sheriff and other deputies know also. All will keep your family and Kate in their thoughts and prayers."

As we chatted, several nurses and doctors, as well as Jim Shanks, the hospital administrator, and Dolly, the hospital receptionist, dropped by to express their support. Kate's best friend, Tina, and her parents, Don and Pauline, came in, followed by John's wife, Cleta, who had her three girls, Scott, and Cameron Madison in tow. We updated them all on the situation.

Their arrival was no surprise since news always spread fast in Kissimmee. When times of trouble rise up in small-town America, so does an enormous support system. Because it was getting late, we encouraged our friends to head home. Pastor Pete prayed, asking for healing for Kate, comfort and peace for us all, and wisdom for John and the rest of Kate's care team.

After everyone left, John came in and took a seat next to mine.

"You look exhausted, John, and very concerned," I said, bracing myself.

"I'll be honest," my colleague replied. "I'm both. But at least Kate's resting, so that's good news. The bad news is that after the third drug, she was still seizing, so I had to begin an infusion with a fourth medication, phenytoin—Dilantin." He turned to my wife. "Barb, Walt knows this, but we use it intravenously for status epilepticus that does not improve with benzodiazepines or phenobarb. The good news is that the Dilantin, or the mixture of all four drugs, finally stopped Kate's convulsions."

Barb took a sharp breath and let it out. "Thank you, Lord!"

"It's also good news that her blood and urine tests are all normal. I performed a lumbar puncture in the ICU, and her spinal fluid is normal, with no sign of elevated pressure, bleeding, or an infection like meningitis. I've ordered an EEG and a brain CT scan. A neurologist has seen her and found no sign of stroke or brain trauma. When all the testing is complete, he'll be back."

John paused for a second as he shifted uncomfortably and cleared his throat. I knew he was extremely concerned. "I must tell you, I'm worried. Her seizure lasted for over ninety minutes, and it took four potent drugs to stop it. She's in a coma and not breathing on her own, hopefully, because of all the medications. The respiratory therapists have her stable on the ventilator. But now it's just a waiting game."

He looked at his watch. "It's almost 10:00 p.m. Why don't you all go home, and I'll call if anything changes."

I glanced at Barb as her eyes welled up. She shook her head. "I need to stay."

"Me too," I added.

John reached out, took our hands, and led us in another prayer. He hugged us both before leaving. We sat and just held each other—lost in our thoughts and prayers.

"I remember writing our medical school friends who were in residency like us when Kate was a one-year-old," Barb said softly.

"It was one of the hardest letters I ever had to write—to tell them about her cerebral palsy diagnosis. People say that babies are life-changing. Well, it's true. Especially if they have a disability like Kate. I shared how her early lack of development concerned us and how you had gone to the medical library and discussed her case with Duke specialists. After dealing by yourself with the shock that she likely had CP, you discussed it with me. Kate had tests, they made the diagnosis, and we began intensive therapy."

"You never told me this before."

"We were both so angry, sorrowful, outraged. You name the emotion, and we experienced it, especially with the name-it-and-claim-it crowd. We cried together and apart. We tried to deal with it ourselves—our grief, our anger at God and each other. You left me alone with Kate. It was bad enough that I felt like people blamed me for Kate's CP, but when you piled on and did the same—"

Barb stopped and blew her nose. "We didn't drift apart; we plummeted apart. Our marriage almost disintegrated, and I came *so* close to leaving you and going home to Baton Rouge."

She wiped her tears and continued. "But God was so good during our storm. He brought friends and neighbors to help us realize Kate was given to us by him as a gift and as a challenge so that others might come to know him through our story and the profound inner beauty of a small but exceptional girl. As we healed, I don't know if we've ever been as close as we became then.

"So when I wrote to our friends to tell them—at that point, she could sit and scoot but wasn't able to crawl, stand, walk, or talk—I said to them that God was giving us enough grace to get through each day and that after a year of dealing with it alone, I needed to tell them about us and how we needed their support and prayers."

Barb reached for my hand and squeezed it gently. "That was about ten years ago, Walt. It seems like time has gone by so quickly. Kate learned to stand, and then she began talking in complete sentences, and then we found out they would mainstream her in school. It turned out her IQ is off the charts, and she's a sweet, wonderful child."

I smiled. "That she is."

"I remember the day I was holding her on my lap after surgery to lengthen some tendons in her legs to make her muscle spasms less disabling. She was wearing a long leg cast and leaned against my chest. She must have heard my heartbeat because she looked up at me and said, 'Momma, I can hear Jesus.' Her eyes were as wide as saucers. 'You can?' I asked. She nodded and said, 'He's making coffee!'"

We both chuckled.

"Her relationship with the Lord is so sweet. She's come so far." Barb's eyes filled with tears. "I've actually begun to dream dreams for her—of college, a career, marriage—that the Lord just might have an amazing plan for her. And now this . . ."

I pulled her close, and we hugged. The door opened, and Dr. Hamp Sessions, the radiologist, entered.

"Walt and Barb, I have results to give you," he said as he sat by us. "Kate's CT is unchanged from when she was little. No evidence of trauma, tumor, infection, or bleeding. She still has a massive hole of water in her brain. She has less than one-third of a right brain and maybe 50 percent of her left brain. It's amazing that she manages half what she does."

I heaved a sigh of relief.

"This is miraculous," Barb said.

Hamp smiled. "I agree. Well, I wanted to tell you in person."

Not long after Hamp left, John returned. "The neurologist ran to an emergency, but we reviewed the EEG together."

"What does it show?" I asked.

John sighed. After Hamp's favorable report, I steeled myself, suspecting that what was coming next was not pleasant news.

"It's a troublesome situation," he began. "Her pupils are fixed and dilated. And her EEG is almost a flat line. She has minimal to no brain waves."

Barb sucked in a deep breath, stiffened, and whispered, "Oh no! Is she brain dead?"

John shook his head. "I don't think so, Barb. Nor does the neurologist. Our hope and prayer is that this is just a drug-induced coma. The combination of her previous brain damage *and* the four powerful medicines could be working together to suppress her breathing and brain activity.

"If we're right, she needs some time for the pharmaceuticals to get out of her system so she can wake up. If or when she does, we can run tests to see if there's been any damage. But given how quickly you got her here and the superb care Ken and Sandi gave her in the ER, I'm very hopeful. She'll likely need to be on an anti-seizure drug for the rest of her life, but I'm praying for a full recovery for her."

I did not share John's optimism. He said her pupils were fixed and dilated, and she had no discernible brain waves. To me, that meant she was clinically dead—and all of our hopes and dreams for her had just evaporated.

I felt like a new black hole had formed in the universe and sucked me in along with my entire world. Not only did all of my revived imaginings, hopes, and expectations for Kate vaporize in an instant but I felt a part of me had died also.

The next twenty-four hours would be crucial.

28

Code Blue, ICU

BARB SENT ME HOME. She *knew* I had a busy day ahead. I wanted to cancel my appointments, but she discouraged it. "While we're waiting, you need to do what you're called to do. Go home. Shower, shave, change clothes, and come back to spell me." She realized I wouldn't nap, and I didn't. But at least I took a shower to freshen up.

When I returned, I sent Barb home to gather some things and take a shower. After checking with Kate's nurse and finding out her situation was stable but unchanged, I made early rounds as the sun was coming up. I went back to the waiting room and was sipping on a coffee when Barb returned and poured a cup. She seemed unusually radiant given our circumstances. "Are you okay?"

"I'm more than okay, Walt," she said as she sat by me. "I just stood in our shower under the stream of hot water, thinking about just how many emotional and spiritual storms we've been through because of Kate's cerebral palsy. God has used her to teach us some painful yet powerful lessons. But it occurred to me that maybe the Lord is also using this to wash us clean."

"What do you mean?"

"So many of our storms have howled or raged—they seem to strike us fast and furious. They don't give us time just to be quiet and heed the still small voice from the Lord. You often say that the same letters form the words *listen* and *silent*. I like that, but I don't often take the time to do that. At home and alone and in the shower, I did."

She took a sip and stared into her coffee. "Although I feel like I'm in one of the worst storms of my life, facing the very real possibility of the death of a fourth child after losing three to miscarriage, I sensed that I did not want this one to get the best of me—to overwhelm, overcome, and overpower me."

My wife looked up. "You know my favorite hymn, don't you?"

"'It Is Well,'" I said.

She nodded. "I looked it up once. A man named Horatio Spafford wrote the hymn in the 1870s. He had gone through some terrible trials in his life. His four-year-old son died. Then the Great Chicago Fire destroyed several of his properties and devastated his finances. Another economic downturn a couple of years later slowed his financial recovery, which kept him from taking a long-planned voyage to Europe with his family, so he sent them ahead.

"During their trans-Atlantic crossing, the ship collided with another and sank in minutes. All four of Spafford's daughters drowned. His wife, Anna, survived and sent him a telegram saying two words: 'Saved alone.' He sailed to meet her, and when his ship passed the location where his four children perished, he wrote the hymn."[1]

Barb began to hum and then softly sing:

> When peace, like a river, attendeth my way,
> When sorrows like sea billows roll;
> Whatever my lot, Thou hast taught me to say,
> It is well; it is well with my soul.[2]

"Walt, I found myself on my knees in the shower. The weight of the pain pulled me down. Then I shocked myself by telling the Lord that Kate was his. I thanked him for giving her to us and for all he had done in our lives because of her. I praised him for her and knew at the bottom of my heart that I could trust, really trust, that he is sovereign in and over *every* circumstance—even the worst imaginable events can only lead to the best because God is in control. Whether he chooses to leave Kate with us or to take her to heaven to be with him, our eternal future is infinitely greater than any pain in our present."

"Wow" was all I could whisper.

"I came to realize there were only two answers to my prayers for her healing. Either she was going to be healed, or she was going to be healed. Either she was going to live, or she was going to live. Either she was going to be with family, or she was going to be with family.

"I instantly knew that we were going to have victory in this situation because of what Jesus has already done for us. Kate staying with us or leaving doesn't change his plan or power or love for us." Barb took a deep breath. "Walt, an incredible peace filled me and washed over me like the hot water. My anxieties and fears washed down the drain, and an image filled my mind. It was the ocean. Sometimes calm and sometimes whipped to foam by squalls and terrible storms, but either way, deep below, there lay pearls of great worth. Does that make sense?"

I nodded. "It does."

"When I stood, I was actually choosing to take a stand to trust him, really trust him, no matter our circumstances or trials or storms."

I put my coffee down and pulled her close. As I did, a verse popped into my head. It was when Jesus told his twelve disciples, "If you love your son or daughter more than me, you are not worthy of being mine."[3]

I was so grateful for this wonderful, amazing woman. My precious wife was entirely worthy of being his.

I went home again to grab a few more things. When I returned, I met Barb in the hospital cafeteria for a bite of breakfast, although neither of us was very hungry. Barb shared that Sandi had taken her into Kate's room.

"I spent time beside Kate. She's still hooked up to the ventilator and all those beeping machines and monitors. Sandi encouraged me to talk, read, and sing to her as the staff did their routine care. I held Kate's hand, prayed with her, and told her how much we loved her. I thanked her for all she had taught us. I gave her permission to go to heaven. I told her we'd see her again. I told her I knew that as sure as anything I had ever believed."

Barb and I walked back to the ICU family waiting room and took our seats while waiting to meet John and the neurologist. Suddenly, alarms sounded, and Dolly, the hospital operator, announced, "Code Blue, ICU. Code Blue, ICU."

Looking out the door, we watched in dread as the code team rushed into Kate's room. We held each other close as a fresh thought flashed. *Lord, I join Barb in surrender. Kate's yours, Lord.* Then I reprimanded myself. *Well, you dummy, she actually always has been the Lord's.*

I sensed an immediate and overwhelming calmness at that moment. Then I realized she had left us, that she died and was in her Father's arms. We had lost our fourth child.

I stared straight ahead, taking this news in, wondering if I should say something to Barb. Then, to my shock and utter amazement, I saw several staff members file out of Kate's room, laughing and slapping each other on the back. We sprinted to her room to see what had happened.

A miracle! Kate had awakened, pulled out her breathing tube, and ripped off the leads to the heart monitor—setting off the alarms leading to the code response. There she was, sitting up and looking bemused as she asked us incredulously, "Why am I not wearing any underwear? And where are my glasses?" Then she added, "And I'm hungry."

Barb and I looked at each other and laughed as tears flooded down our faces.

"It's a miracle!" Barb said.

"It *is* a miracle," John said as he walked up behind us and put his arms around our shoulders.

Kate's friends couldn't visit her in the ICU, but all day long, they came to her ground-floor ICU room window. The neurologist pronounced her back to baseline—meaning no evidence of any harm from her prolonged seizure.

Her only complaint? "I feel like a truck hit me!" she exclaimed, a not-so-surprising claim given the nearly two hours of constant muscle contractions all over her body due to the seizure.

"Nothing that warm baths, stretching and moving, along with gentle massages, acetaminophen, and ibuprofen won't take care of," John advised. He moved her to a hospital room to finish her loading doses of an oral anti-seizure drug that she would have to take the rest of her life. John did not want to discharge her until she was stable and the medication was at the proper level in her system. Tina never left Kate's side and rode home from the hospital with us.

When I returned home from the office late that afternoon, I hugged and kissed both girls. Tina, ever the plainspoken one, said, "Dr. Walt, have you gained some weight?"

"I plead the Fifth Amendment," I said as I turned to join Barb in the kitchen, chuckling as the girls began reciting lines of the poem "Bustopher Jones" from T. S. Eliot's book *Old Possum's Book of Practical Cats*. Bustopher was a plump feline from the St. James's Street section of London, an area known for many upper-class clubs that the cat frequented, and was *very* well fed.[4]

Kate began reciting, and Tina picked up with another verse. They continued back and forth until the girls howled in laughter. Barb hugged me with tears of joy streaking down her cheeks. "She's back!"

I remember Bill teaching me to look for God's fingerprints in every trial and God's rainbow at the end of every tempest. The final chapter of any journey the Lord leads us on will be joyous.

For Barb and me, it was good to see a brilliantly bright rainbow.

PART THREE

Perfect Gifts after Storms

When you come out of the storm, you
won't be the same person who walked in.
That's what this storm's all about.

Haruki Murakami, *Kafka on the Shore*

29

The Prank

THERE WAS A KNOCK ON THE FRONT DOOR. I was surprised to see Officer Gib Michaels carrying an evidence box. "How can I help you, Gib?"

"Doc, is your son here?"

"Is there a problem?"

"There may well be."

"Please, come in," I said, opening the door wider. "I'll get him."

The three of us sat down in the family room. Scott, twelve at the time, looked nervous and fidgety.

"Remember when I made you a junior officer for the Kissimmee Police Department?" Gib began.

"Yes, sir," Scott answered, looking at the floor.

When he was a little boy, Scott had called 9-1-1 to see what would happen. Officer Michaels came to investigate.

"Back then, I told your father I hoped you understood the difference between right and wrong. Do you remember that?"

Scott nodded, and his head remained slumped. I wondered where this was going.

"You also told me you wouldn't take part in any more pranks, correct?"

Scott continued to nod.

Gib reached into his box and pulled out a package. "Scott, do you recognize this?"

Scott looked up briefly and shook his head.

"It's a partially filled box of girls' panty liners. Have you seen it before?"

Scott did not reply.

Gib reached down and pulled a backpack out of the box. "Scott, one of our detectives found this backpack. Do you recognize it?"

Scott looked up again. His eyes widened, and his lips tensed. "Yes, sir. I do."

"Is it yours?"

Scott nodded as his head dropped.

Gib showed me the name tag on the backpack, which read, "Scott Larimore." He looked at my son. "Scott, the empty panty liner box was in your backpack. We found it on the path from the house your family rented until you moved here. Some pranksters took a bunch of panty liners and stuck them on the garage door of the house across the street. They also placed them on the truck outside. The garage door message said HELLO, and the truck door notice spelled HI. Both with block letters. Do you know who did this?"

"Yes, sir."

"Who was in on this with you?" Gib asked.

Scott whispered the names of his coconspirators.

Suddenly, everything made sense to me. Scott and his friends had asked to camp in our backyard the Friday night before. They must have sneaked off.

"Did this happen Friday night, Gib?" I asked.

"They reported it to us on Saturday, so I'd have to say yes. We couldn't identify any fingerprints, and there were no security cameras on the house. But we found this evidence—your son's backpack. Chief Ross allowed me to come over here. He wanted to keep it in the family, if you know what I mean. Especially given the damage."

"Damage?!" Scott and I exclaimed.

Gib nodded. "The adhesive on the panty liners is fine for cloth or skin but quite damaging to paint. It caused the garage and truck door paint to blister, and repainting both will be expensive. The family's daughter suspected you guys were the culprits. The family knows and likes you boys. If you make full restitution, they have agreed not to press charges, and the police department will drop the case. That is, once we're notified that you restored everything to its original condition, and it is acceptable to the family."

"Scott," I said, "is that agreeable?"

"Yes, sir."

"And that will also mean replacing the panty liners you stole from your sister, young man."

We talked and came up with a plan that Gib considered acceptable.

———

That evening, at our family dinner, we had a fruitful discussion about both stealing and damaging others' property—and the cost of poor decision-making. Scott agreed to the plan we had come up with, which I believed was both biblical and wise.

Scott first had to admit his mistake to himself, Officer Michaels, Barb and me, and then the Lord. I explained that the Bible promises that God is faithful and just to forgive our wrongs and cleanse us from all unrighteousness if we admit our mistakes to ourselves, acknowledge them to God and those we harm, and choose to go another direction in the future.[1] This type of confession is like having our dirty slate wiped clean spiritually.

Second, Scott and I needed to go to his friends and talk with them and their parents. They would need to agree with our plan.

Third, we all needed to go to the family whose property had

been damaged and talk to them—to agree on making things right and ask for forgiveness.

Last, Scott would have to do some significant work to make money for the expensive repairs.

That night at bedtime, I went to spend some time with my son. I told him I wasn't happy with what he had done, but I admired his courage.

"Anyone can make a mistake," I told him. "I've sure made plenty and likely have plenty ahead. But it takes a real man to admit when he's done wrong, face the consequences, and make it right. All men make mistakes; wise men learn from them."

"Right, Dad."

"What's one thing you can do to make me or your mom or the Lord love you more?" That was my favorite of two questions I liked to ask and emphasize to my children.

He grinned. "Nothing."

"That's correct. And what's one thing you can do to make us love you less?"

"Nothing."

I gave him an enormous hug. "Scott, your mom and I totally forgive you. You don't have to lug guilt around. You can let it go. Instead of carrying mistakes like millstones around your neck, use them as stepping-stones to a better future and a better you. Make sense?"

We hugged again and said a bedtime prayer.

Repainting the garage door and fixing the truck did turn out to be expensive. I seem to remember that each boy's family had to pay five hundred dollars to restore the damaged property. Scott had to do many extra chores for the next two months— pulling weeds, mowing the lawn, and washing the dishes after dinner. He wasn't allowed to play with his friends as often as he wanted.

But that was okay. I'm proud to say that the cost of learning a lesson has stayed with my son to this day.

30

The Unkindest Cut

"Dad! Mom!" Yelps of sobbing followed Scott's screams from outside. "Help!" he wailed.

Barb and I leaped from the breakfast table and sprinted out the door to the garage. Scott squatted by his bike. He was in a T-shirt, shorts, and flip-flops. To our horror, under his leg, a pool of bright red blood was growing as blood oozed from behind his knee onto the concrete.

"I cut my leg on the bike sprocket!" he cried. "I almost cut my leg off!" He continued to sob uncontrollably. He was white. I quickly laid him down and examined the back of his knee. There were spurts of blood coming from several small arteries. I tried to remain calm.

"Barb, grab a clean towel. Now!"

She turned and ran to the kitchen.

"Scott, let's roll you onto your stomach." The wound was awful, extending deep into the space behind the knee—the popliteal fossa. I could easily see two major blood vessels, two large nerves, the two heads of the major calf muscle, and the three tendons from the major thigh muscle. Thankfully, they were intact, but honestly,

I felt like I was back in gross anatomy lab or looking at an illustration of the popliteal fossa in *Gray's Anatomy*.

"Here!" Barb handed me a clean towel, and I used it to apply direct pressure, which controlled the bleeding.

"Call the ER to let them know we're coming." Barb returned to the house while I helped Scott to the car and laid him on the back seat while holding pressure on the wound.

"I was taking my bike down when I tripped," Scott told me. "Somehow, my leg went through the bike and across the sprocket. It hurts *so* bad!"

Barb returned and we screeched out of the driveway. "We'll be at the ER in a few minutes," I reassured Scott.

Dr. Byerly and Sandi met us as we entered the ER's back door. We put Scott on a gurney and rolled him into the treatment room. Ken examined the wound. The bleeding was now minimal due to the direct pressure.

"Thank the Lord!" he said. "Another few millimeters and you could have sliced any or all of the tendons, nerves, or the popliteal artery and vein."

"Amen," was all I could say.

"Want me to call John?"

"He's out of town," I said. "How about you and I work on this together, Ken?"

"We're pretty busy here. I know Dr. Gonzales has just finished an emergency appendectomy. How about I call him?"

"Sounds great. I'd appreciate some help."

"I'll assist," Sandi added. "You'll need an extra set of hands."

While we waited for Pete, I pulled up a stool to sit by Scott. "How are you feeling?"

He sniffled. "It still hurts a lot, Dad. Not as bad as earlier though."

I rubbed his head. "I'm proud of you, Scott. But once we get it numbed up and closed, you're going to feel a whole lot better. I promise."

He smiled. "Thanks, Dad. I'm just glad you were there for me."

"Me too, buddy."

———

It took a while for Dr. Gonzales and me to complete the repair. First we had to work from our respective sides, toward the middle of the gaping wound, numbing it with several generous injections of lidocaine mixed with epinephrine. The lidocaine was the anesthetic; the epinephrine constricted the small arteries to stem any more bleeding. We cleaned the grease in and around the deep laceration and rinsed the wound with two liters of normal saline.

"The solution to pollution . . ." Dr. Pete began, quoting an old axiom of surgery.

"Is dilution with solution," I said, completing the saying.

We each chuckled and prepped the wound with Betadine antiseptic, applied sterile drapes, and then began sewing from the inside out. We both placed a deep and superficial layer of absorbable interrupted ligatures using durable suture material.

"Putting in a couple of drains would be wise," Pete said.

I nodded. I knew they would create a channel to allow any blood or fluid collecting in the popliteal space to drain, helping reduce the risk of infection and promote more rapid healing. Finally, we placed strong skin sutures.

"How many sutures?" Pete asked Sandi.

She looked at the instrument tray. She had used a surgical marker to keep count. "Looks like forty on the inside and another fifteen on the outside."

"How about tetanus and antibiotic shots?" Pete asked Sandi. She left to get them.

Pete turned to me. "I'll also write a script for an oral antibiotic for ten days and some pain meds. We'll apply a bulky dressing, an ACE bandage for compression, and a leg immobilizer to keep the knee from bending for a few days. I'll get Sandi to fit some crutches for him and give him directions on how to use them. I'd recommend pulling the drains in three to four days and then begin physical therapy to keep the scar from contracting and preventing full knee extension."

I nodded. As Scott's dad, I'm not sure I would have thought of all these items of standard quality care. I find it challenging to be a family member and a doctor at the same time. Some doctors can do it, but I am not one of them, and maybe that is a good thing. As Sir William Osler famously wrote more than a hundred years ago, "The doctor who treats himself has a fool for a patient."[1]

No wonder the American Medical Association says, "In general, physicians should not treat themselves or members of their own families" with one prominent exception: "In emergency settings or isolated settings where there is no other qualified physician available. In such situations, physicians should not hesitate to treat themselves or their family members until another physician becomes available."[2]

Scott went to bed early that night. Kate, Barb, and I shared some ice cream and were debriefing about the day when Kate said, "Mom and Dad, I need to confess something. I was watching TV in the family room when I heard Scott's cries. I didn't do anything because I thought he was just joking, as he often does. I hope you're not angry with me."

Barb tried to suppress a chuckle.

"What?" Kate asked.

"I ignored his cries too," she said. "When I first heard him, I thought he was frustrated with his bike, crying wolf. But his second cry was different. It was from his gut, and I knew something was wrong."

"Like father, like son," I added.

"What do you mean?" Kate said.

"All of the Larimore men are kind of known as jokesters. It runs in the family."

"Your dad and brothers are," Barb said. "That's for sure."

"It goes way back," I said. "According to family lore, when my ancestor James Larimore was twenty, he emigrated from Ireland in 1760 with two of his brothers. Every subsequent generation of the Larimore clan has been known for 'boisterous lighthearted boys.' Jimmy was just the first of many."

"So, you're saying you inherited your joking nature?"

I nodded. "But it can be dangerous if you're not careful."

"How?" Kate asked.

"Old family tradition records that Jimmy was a great tease. He would often come home, hopping around, claiming that he had been bitten by a rattlesnake or something else. It kept his wife, Susannah, in a constant state of fear. Finally, she quit paying attention to his jokes and bluffs."

"And?" Kate asked.

"Well, this is the sad part. The family legend is that at seventy-seven years of age, he was actually bitten by a rattler while climbing over a log in the forest. At first, his wife didn't believe him, so she didn't treat him. He swelled up and died."[3]

"Wow," Kate said, "I guess you're saying that if you're going to cry wolf, be careful who you cry to and be careful how often you do so, right?'

I gave her a hug. "I think your brother and I both have learned a lesson. Constant joking, like chronic lying, can sometimes result in the loss of the trust of others."

———

The next day, Dr. Gonzales and his wife came by the house. Pete removed Scott's leg immobilizer and bandages. To our relief, there was almost no drainage from the wounds and no sign of infection.

"I think applying antibiotic ointment and a large nonstick bandage should be enough. Do you have what we need?" he asked.

I thought a moment, had an idea pop into my head, and laughed. After locating the ointment, Kate and her friend Tina, who was over visiting, helped me find what I was looking for—the *perfect* Band-Aid.

Coming back to Scott's room with Kate and Tina, I handed Pete the ointment, and he slathered it on the wound. I then opened a box and gave him the next item to cover the injury.

His and Scott's eyes widened.

"Oh no, Dad!" Scott exclaimed.

"That's not what I think it is?" Pete asked.

I nodded, and Pete laughed. "My, oh my. It's perfect! Who would have thought a panty liner would work so well for this!"

Of course, women know that the liners have many practical uses. We males had never heard of *any* of these ideas. Kate, Tina, Cleta, and Barb named off just a few: absorbent insoles for high heel shoes, an inexpensive alternative to makeup wipes, sweat protection for the underarms of shirts, convenient wipes for nail polish remover, an economical alternative to nursing pads, a cleaner pad for computer screens, and a quick and straightforward protection pad for furniture legs. My favorite of all their ideas: drawer fresheners!

What was one of the most expensive ways to use them? Scott and his friends had found out the hard way by sticking them to a garage door and truck!

I'm pleased to say that the panty liners did their job and helped heal Scott's hurting leg. With each dressing change, I chuckled. The Lord sure has interesting ways to teach each of us life lessons.

31

By-and-By

GEECH'S HEART DISEASE took a turn for the worse, and before long, he was bedridden at his ranch. Whenever I would visit him, he'd tell more and more of the remarkable history and culture of Osceola County. It wasn't unusual for him to quip, "You'd understand all this a lot better if you were from around here."

"Geech, quit rubbing it in!" I said, pretending to be offended. "Right now, you're the best teacher I've got to learn all this."

His treasure trove of memories about all things "cowboy" and "local" was seemingly inexhaustible. His jokes and wry sense of humor always left us both chuckling. He'd laugh—my goodness, how I loved his laugh.

Dan Autrey, his brother-in-law, took my favorite picture of him at their hunting camp out in the wilderness. In the picture, Geech is breaking out in a belly-shaking cackle.

"Old friends, timeworn tales, and jokes—it don't get much better than that," Geech would say, picking up the frame to view a younger version of himself. He mixed laughter with warmhearted memories and sage advice, which were deeply deposited in my memory bank and character. Geech was all the proof I needed regarding King Solomon's wise proverb, "Being cheerful keeps you healthy."[1] He was happy and content, not because everything in his life was always good—it wasn't—but because he chose to find the good side of everything life sent his way.

One Sunday afternoon, Scott and I hopped in my truck to visit Geech. I wondered if this would be the last time we'd see each other this side of heaven. As we parked, Connie and their daughter, Kathy, came out to meet us.

"Doc," Kathy said, "glad you're here. We don't think he has much more time. I'm upping his pain medication, which makes him comfortable, but he's sleeping longer and longer."

The news confirmed my suspicions. "Are you all still okay with him staying here?"

"It's what he wants, Doc," Connie assured me. "He was born on his daddy's ranch, and he prefers to pass here on his own."

"I'll notify the coroner," I said. "When the time comes, either call Dr. John or me, and we'll let the funeral home know. Shall we go see him?"

They nodded, and we went inside. Several family members were gathered in the dining and living rooms. I greeted them all and admired the half-finished chalk mural that Connie, who had been trained in art at the Ringling School of Arts in Sarasota, placed on the thick horsehair plaster of her dining room wall. On the right section was the lakeshore, lined with a small group of palm trees. I had never noticed this feature before. I glanced out the picture window at the back of the house, and sure enough, a healthy grove bordered the lake.

"That's Geech's daddy, Henry Partin—my granddaddy," Kathy explained, pointing to the older man depicted in the middle of the mural. "He's wearing his old Stetson and the tan pants he always wore. Never did wear jeans, and I don't know why. Look at his left hand. See anything strange?"

I squinted, examining the figure. "Does he have some arthritis?"

"Well, yes. But he doesn't have a little finger. Lost it when a gun he was shooting backfired and blew it off," she said matter-of-factly. "Behind him are some of his famed Brahman cattle."

Connie jumped in. "Geech's daddy's Heart Bar Ranch was the largest privately owned ranch east of the Mississippi in the 1950s," she explained. "He brought the first Brahman cattle to the state from Texas in the 1930s, and the Partins became well known in the ranching industry as breeders of Brahman cattle. In fact, the ranch eventually became the headquarters for Brahman cattle in Florida."

Standing off to the side in the mural was a grazing horse. "That's Princess Misty and her colt," Connie said. "That colt was one of Geech's last horses. He called him Goober. Just buried him out by the barn not too long ago."

"Looks like a Quarter Horse."

Connie laughed. "Doc, you're beginning to learn our ways. Yep, he was. Geech loves the breed, owned the first one in Florida, and became one of the founding members of the American Quarter Horse Association."

"On the other side of the painting is Daddy," Kathy said. I could see the outline of a partially drawn cowboy, appearing to observe his father and the stock from a distance.

"I just can't seem to get his nose just right," Connie commented. "Hope to finish it someday."

"You know," Kathy added, "his nose was broken quite a few times."

I had always noticed that feature of his face but never inquired whether it was from bucking bulls, broncs, or the knuckles of a furious challenger or cowhand.

We walked into the bedroom. The hospice nurse updated me on Geech's condition and medications. I checked the medicine cabinet, the oxygen concentrator, and the IVs—all of which were in perfect order. A wall clock, with a pendulum slowly moving back and forth below it, clicked away the seconds.

"That old clock reminds me of the ones I saw when I practiced in the Smoky Mountains," I said. "When I would be called to a home to pronounce a loved one dead, I would usually find that a family member, usually the spouse or oldest child, had stopped the clock the moment someone took their last breath."

Connie nodded. "The pioneers believed that when one passed away, time would stop for that person as they entered their timeless eternity. They thought that allowing a ticking timepiece would invite the deceased's spirit to stay. Stopping the clock and placing a black cloth over it was their way of giving the spirit of the dead permission to move on."

"In Bryson City, it was helpful to me because I could record that time on the death certificate."

"And we put that time in the family Bible."

I pulled up a chair by Geech's hospital bed. As he breathed slowly, I examined him. His lungs had the classic clatter that is called the *death rattle*. His pulse was slow but regular, and he appeared comfortable. As I sat back, the chair creaked, and he opened his eyes, blinking several times to clear his vision.

"How are you doing, Geech?" I asked.

"Fair to middling." He reached out for my hand and softly said, "Doc, pretty soon, I think I'm nearing my last ride. You know that, don't 'cha?"

I nodded. "I suspect you're right."

I knew from experience that patients often were aware of these things long before their family would acknowledge or admit the end was near.

Geech smiled—*that* smile—and I perceived some jest or special memory was coming. In this case, it was the latter.

"I always loved how Clem would end his prayer at the beginning of each rodeo. He'd say, 'Help us, Lord, to live our lives in such a manner that when we make that last inevitable ride to the country up there, where the grass grows lush, green, and stirrup high, and where the water runs cool, clear, and deep, that you, as our last Judge, will tell us that our entry fees are paid.'"[2]

"I suspect yours have already been taken care of, my friend," I said.

"I'm hoping I'll get to meet your grandpappy. If he's at all like you, I suspect I'm gonna like him."

I was deeply touched. Geech was not jesting at all. Instead, this patriarch of our county had declared that his family doctor was now "from here" or "one of us"—a bona fide "local." It was about as high an honor as a physician for cowboys can ever get.

"Would it be time for us to say goodbye?" I asked.

He shook his head. "Nope. Cowboys don't ever say goodbye. It's not in our nature. I prefer that old hymn . . ."

His voice broke and faded. Then he smiled. "I'll see you in that sweet by-and-by."

I nodded. "I like that better."

"Me too," he whispered. "Me too."

He tried to reposition himself. The pain caused him to grimace ever so slightly, but he didn't make a sound—cowboys don't.

My years as the rodeo doctor taught me there's a vast difference between the average man and a genuine, cattle-working, rodeo cowboy like Geech. I took care of them, but I wasn't one of them—I could never have been. I remember him telling me once, "Cowboys are pretty tough on the outside, but the really good ones are sweet and soft on the inside, like a week-old cream-filled doughnut!"

"You need some pain medication, Mr. Partin?" the hospice nurse asked.

He shook his head. "Naw. It ain't as bad as a poke in the eye with a sharp stick. But this trying to roll over with my bad back is 'bout as easy as putting socks on a rooster. Both'll give a man a hurtin'."

His eyes glimmered. "Doc, I've found that in life, pain is inevitable. Moaning about it is optional. A true cowboy knows a lot about love and pain. I've found I prefer the former to the latter," he said. "But 'cha gotta learn to live with both."

He thought a moment, and then, with a twinkle in his eyes, he added, "When you're young and you fall off a horse, you may break something. When you're my age, you splatter."

The nurse and I both smiled as we helped reposition him.

I tried to lift his spirits. "If I had a dime for every cowboy saying you ever told me, I'd be a rich man."

"You actually are richer just because you heard 'em." Geech chuckled. "But if you had a quarter for every one of 'em that was worth a hoot, you couldn't get a dollar bill."

I smiled. "I'm still a rich man."

"You bring your boy?" Geech asked.

I nodded.

"Hey, Scott," he called out. "You there? You all right?"

Scott walked over. "I am, Mr. Partin."

"I still laugh when I think about the day that nasty old rodeo bull almost ran over your daddy. Remember that?"

Scott smiled. "I do, Mr. Partin. 'Bout scared Scott Ramsey and me to death."

"Not as bad as it scared your daddy. I swear I don't know how he kept from wetting his pants!" Geech quipped. "Have you met Wrinkles?"

Scott looked confused and shook his head.

"My favorite bull of all times. He's nearly 1,500 pounds and looks and acts as mean as a riled-up junkyard dog, but he's not. Follows me everywhere like a puppy dog when I scoot around the pastures. Anyway, one cow carrying an offspring of his is about to calf out in the barn. He's watching guard from outside. I'd like you to meet him. But I don't want you bidding on him. He ain't for sale."

Scott and I smiled. We were both thinking back on our purchase of LA a few years earlier.

"I'd like to meet Wrinkles, Mr. Partin."

Geech grinned. "Connie, will you take Doc and his boy to meet him?"

"Love to," she replied.

"You mind if I pray with you before we head out?" I asked.

"Nope. But if we could do it with the rest of my family, that would be nice. Some of 'em need to find their way back to the Lord. I should know. I wandered in that lonely pasture myself for many a year."

Kathy called in the family, who gathered around the bed.

Geech whispered to me, "They look about as uncomfortable as a rooster in a pond."

Then from his bed, he looked up and spoke to his kin, "This here's the best doctor I've had the last few years," he boasted. A wry smile spread the sun-worn wrinkles across his face. "'Course, he's the only doc I've had the last few years, so I guess he's the worst one also!"

We all heard that laugh of his. I loved it—and him.

We all held hands. On one side of me was Geech, my hand wrapped in his. My other hand gripped Scott's. I don't remember what I prayed, but it was short, and it must have been meaningful. His eyes were moist as he clasped my hand and pulled me down close.

"Don't tell no one we held hands!" he whispered, but everyone heard him and smiled at this special man.

I can still see him in my mind.

Connie walked Scott and me toward their big red barn. Just beside it was a massive bull that was pacing back and forth. I had seen this type of behavior in the maternity care waiting room of humans more times than I could count, with men who either didn't want to or could not be in the birthing room. A forlorn bellowing came from inside the barn.

"Must be close!" Connie said as we picked up our pace.

In a stall on a thick mat of fresh hay, we found the cow faced away from us, lifting her tail to reveal a half-birthed calf.

"It's not the usual time for calving," Connie remarked, "but it'll delight Geech she's having another for him and Wrinkles before he passes. That'll tickle him to death." She laughed. "Guess I shouldn't say it that way, should I?"

"I think it's just perfect, Connie," I said.

"Here, Scott," Connie said, pointing. "Come stand up on the railing. You ever seen a calf born?"

Scott shook his head and stepped up on the lower rail. Connie walked up behind him.

"Here it comes," she whispered as the cow and Wrinkles both bellowed in unison and the calf plopped out onto the cushioned floor. The cow spun around and began licking the amniotic sac off the calf's face as it snorted and coughed. In only a few seconds, the newborn struggled to its feet as the doting mother continued to cleanse it.

"I'm happy to see a healthy calf," Connie whispered. "It's the way of a ranch. Birth, life, death. It's the cycle of life. I guess we're all on the same journey."

"It's amazing and beautiful," Scott whispered, his eyes transfixed on the scene.

As we left the barn, we stood, spellbound, listening to the sandhill cranes' cackling songs and watching a spectacular Florida sunset over the lake.

"I remember when I was a little girl," Connie said, "I learned a Bible verse I've always loved: 'From the rising of the sun to the place where it sets, the name of the LORD is to be praised.'"[3] She took a deep breath and let it out slowly, adding, "From first breath until last."

As we said our goodbyes, Connie gave me a long hug. "You're a blessing."

"Connie, I'm the one who has been blessed." I tried to blink the tears away. "If I don't hear from you by tomorrow evening, I'll pop by to check on him." I knew in my heart I would not have to return.

As we headed home through the picturesque countryside and

cool evening, Scott and I were lost in our thoughts. The juxta-position of a waning life well lived and a new existence ready to begin was a powerful reminder for me of just how short a period we each have.

Scott unbuckled his seat belt and scooted over to sit by me. He rested his head on my chest, and I put my arm around his shoulders. He sniffled, and I pulled him close. As he wiped his tears, I asked, "You sad?"

"Some," he said, "for Mrs. Connie and Kathy and Coach Baker and their family. But I'm happy for Mr. Partin. He'll soon be in heaven and won't have any more pain or tears, will he?"

"It's a great promise we all have, isn't it, Scott?"

He sniffled and looked up at me. "What a blessing."

"What? To know we will all be together with the Lord in heaven one day?"

"Well, that. But mainly that you get to be a family doctor!"

Tears again formed in my eyes, and I could only nod. I was indeed blessed.

I was learning the universal truth that God blesses each of us with both laughter and tears. Life is merriment and melancholy mixed together, a journey accompanied by happiness and heart-ache, delights and despair. As a younger man, I had trouble understanding King Solomon's declaration, "Sorrow is better than laughter, for sadness has a refining influence on us."[4] Now it was beginning to make sense.

As Geech would say, "God deals with us as gently as he can or as harshly as he must." Another time he told me, "Real life ain't really easy! It's like bucking stock. They want to throw you down to the ground. But every time you're tossed off, you're closer to the joy of that perfect eight-second ride."

His prescription to all for a healthy heart and soul was this: "Just be what the Lord's leading you to be—then you can be your true self. Be real, be an original, hold on tight, and enjoy the ride. God never said that the journey would be easy, but he promises that in the end, the arrival will be worthwhile."

I was beginning to grasp his meaning. In real life, a life lived faithfully and fully is full of bliss and burden, delight and distress, glee and gloom, along with pain and pleasure. Each of these counterparts walks hand in hand.

While the welcomed and wanted events can be fulfilling, the unwelcome and unwanted ones cannot be avoided. But both can be celebrated to create a real me. It is the only explanation for the commandment, "Consider it a sheer gift, friends, when tests and challenges come at you from all sides. You know that under pressure, your faith-life is forced into the open and shows its true colors. So don't try to get out of anything prematurely. Let it do its work, so you become mature and well-developed, not deficient in any way."[5]

It is good advice for any of us on our journey through life.[6]

32

Lady in Red

BARB AND I SHARED THE DESIRE to have a large family—that we might bless our children, and they us, and so we could leave behind a godly heritage. We understood that not all parents received this call, but we both sensed and responded to it.

After Kate and Scott were born, we lost four babies in a row to miscarriage (one in Bryson City and three in Kissimmee, including one after Kate's seizure). Each conception began a journey that we neither expected nor desired.

After the conception of each tiny unborn child came ultrasounds, showing what appeared to be healthy little ones—moving, kicking, squirming, hiccoughing, and thumb sucking. Their minuscule size didn't keep us from falling head over heels in love with each one. "Because after all, a person's a person, no matter how small," as Dr. Seuss so eloquently proclaimed in *Horton Hears a Who*.[1]

With each pint-sized person myriad hopes and aspirations arose in our hearts. We felt each child move and kick—what we physicians call *quickening*, the moment in pregnancy when the woman feels or perceives her unborn baby stirring in her womb.

The word *quick* originally meant "alive." We prayed for each

201

child and discussed potential names. Our families and friends shared our joy and excitement over each unborn child, and Kate and Scott were old enough to share our excitement as well. Our spirits soared in mounting anticipation and expectation.

And then, with each pregnancy came a day when Barb could no longer sense our baby moving. The dreaded ultrasounds that followed showed no heartbeat, and blood tests indicated plummeting levels of the pregnancy hormone, hCG (human chorionic gonadotropin). Both would confirm what our hearts knew to be true—another death.

What followed each loss was a season of indescribable agony, angst, and anguish. The surprise to me, as a physician, was how each subsequent loss became more painful and challenging than the one before and how each became more excruciating—a phenomenon I found in the years that followed that my patients also experienced with child loss.

Each death of a child was a blow to our hearts that weighed our spirits down, close to the point of snapping. But even worse, the weight and burden of each subsequent loss was increasingly unbearable for both of us but especially for Barb.

Friends prayed early and often that the Lord would protect the life and health of our last unborn baby, but God's answer was, "No. I'll take this one to heaven with me." With the fourth loss, life nearly stopped.

John recommended we take some time to ourselves while our friends Jerry and Jennifer Adamson booked a several-day stay for us at the Lakeside Inn of Mount Dora, known in guidebooks as "Florida's Most Historic Hotel."[2] They even volunteered to keep Kate and Scott.

Mount Dora, forty-five miles north of Kissimmee, has been a longtime haven for artists and antique lovers. The inn was originally built as a ten-room structure in 1883, and it opened during the Victorian era when leisure activities like bird-watching, fishing, picnicking, picking oranges and grapefruit, and reading were all the rage. The inn survived as one of Florida's few historic wooden hostelries and as the oldest continuously operating hotel in Florida. Guests could relax by the pool or on the two-hundred-foot-long veranda that was lined with comfortable white rocking chairs and watch stunning sunsets over Lake Dora.[3]

As Barb and I walked through the stone entry gates, we stepped back in time as we beheld the large moss-draped oak trees and acres of beautifully landscaped grounds. We were looking forward to the possibility of taking in some sunbathing and swimming, bird-watching and nature walks, and shopping and antiquing. I had secretly booked a guided boat tour and an after-dinner carriage ride. I knew Barb would mostly want some time to read, pray, and just contemplate in a comfortable rocking chair. I was hoping for a time of simple pleasures, shared and enjoyed with the love of my life in this romantic, classic, and lovely inn.

For our first evening, I had reserved a table at the inn's fine-dining Beauclaire Dining Room. Brochure photographs showed a beautiful room with a crescent of enormous windows that featured picturesque garden views. In an era long before Tripadvisor, friends said the Beauclaire provided a gracious dining experience in elegant surroundings with superb service. Barb deserved no less.

After a tour of the grounds, a swim, and some lounging by the poolside, we took a nap then prepared for dinner. As I was waiting for Barb, I read a book and listened to an easy-listening music station. When Barb stepped out, she looked radiant in a new red dress with a plunging neckline. She spun around, flashing her gorgeous smile. "How do I look?"

I was speechless and walked over just to hold her. "Honey, you've never looked as dazzling as you do tonight," I said as we began to slow dance. "Never so radiant, never so bright," I whispered in her ear as the incredibly romantic song, "The Lady in Red," sung by Chris de Burgh, played in the background.

"You're a poet and don't know it," she said, chuckling.

"A beautiful lady in a spectacular dress," I said, pulling her close.

"It's new," she whispered. "Just for you. Well, it's for us. A new dress for a new start."

"The lady in red is dancing with me," I half hummed, half murmured. "There's nowhere else I'd rather be than with you."

Tears streaked down Barb's face. "Now look what you've done. You've made me cry. I'll have to redo my makeup." She rested her head on my shoulder as we embraced. "In a little while. But right now, I just want to be with you."

I pulled away slightly just to gaze at this beautiful woman. "You take my breath away. You are amazing, babe."

"Can we stay here forever?" she whispered.

I'm not sure I've ever had such a wonderful assortment of feelings at the same moment—head over heels, complete, and absolute love for an astonishing woman.

She is a gift to me from God—my lady in red.

———

Later that night, after Barb fell asleep, I was writing in my journal. I pulled out my Bible and began searching for the word *red*. I remembered that some believed the most significant color in the Bible is red because it's the color of blood. The Old Testament sacrifices and, in particular, Jesus's sacrifice on the cross use the imagery of actual shed blood. Because of this, red symbolizes not just death but also sacrifice, atonement, forgiveness, and life. As I thought about it, I sensed that, at least for me, the color red symbolizes the love of God.

That weekend was the beginning of the end of a period of dark, dreary days for us. As God had promised, "I will turn their mourning into joy. I will comfort them and exchange their sorrow for rejoicing."[4] As our sorrow and grief slowly subsided, our God met us in fresh ways. He saw and gathered our tears.[5] He drew near,[6] held us close,[7] and whispered, "Blessed are you who weep now."[8]

I was reassured to see in Scripture a Father God who feels sorrow and even weeps for the wounds and blows, both emotional and physical, of his people. Scripture tells me God's "eyes pour out tears" when his "dear, dear people are battered and bruised,"[9] and, "the LORD is close to the brokenhearted; he rescues those whose spirits are crushed."[10] Another version of the same verse says, "If your heart is broken, you'll find God right there; if you're kicked in the gut, he'll help you catch your breath."[11]

Scripture paints a beautiful picture of a heavenly Father who expresses powerful emotions such as anger[12] and rejoicing,[13] as well as compassion,[14] sadness,[15] and yes, even grief,[16] all covered with the icing of his love, the core of his character.[17]

It comforted me to think he wept as we did over our losses and now rejoiced with us as we, not knowing what our future held, were confident and trusting in him, the one who held our future and us in his hands.

What I didn't realize was that my lady in red had some huge unanswered questions in her heart.[18]

33

Misery to Ministry

A WEEK OR TWO LATER, we shared dinner with Bill and Jane Judge. Barb looked at the Judges during dessert and suddenly asked a question that must have been troubling her heart for some time: "Do you think our miscarried children went to heaven?"

I was proud of her courage in asking. Jane answered, "Oh, honey, of course they did!"

"How do you know?" Barb asked, her eyes getting misty. "Is there anything in the Bible that says this?"

Bill nodded. "I think the best example is the story of David's son, who was conceived out of adultery with Bathsheba. The Bible says the Lord 'struck' the child, and it became ill. For seven days, David fasted and prayed the child would live, but he died. Following his baby's death, David washes, eats, and worships. When asked why he was acting this way, he said, 'He is dead. Why should I fast? Can I bring him back again? I shall go to him, but he will not return to me.'"[1] Bill took a deep breath. "Barb, to me, it's clear that David is saying he will see his infant son in heaven."

"But is that just true for King David's baby?" Barb asked. "How about our babies?"

206

Bill's voice showed no irritation with the challenge to his answer—only warmth and compassion. "Let me explain what I've learned about God's character on this matter. The Bible tells us God creates *all* human beings in his image. Every individual ever conceived bears this image, right from the instant of conception. Even when just a single cell, the microscopic baby is fully human and carries God's image. We know this because the Bible tells us that before God forms us in the womb, he knows us."[2]

"But what about sin?" Barb asked. "What about the psalm that says we are sinful from the time of conception and at birth?[3] Can an unborn baby or young child go to heaven if they don't know Jesus?"

"By all means, yes!" Bill answered.

"How?" Tears formed in her eyes. "How can we be sure?"

Barb signaled to me that she wanted the handkerchief I always carried in my pocket.

"The simple answer is that young children have not rejected Jesus," Bill said, "so I believe his sacrifice covers them—as does his love. At death, they immediately pass into God's presence. We will see them again."

Barb breathed a sigh of relief, and I saw a glimmer of a smile. "One last question that I've been pondering is this: When I see our babies in heaven, will they be babies or children or grown-ups?"

"Well," Bill began, "the Bible doesn't say for sure, but I believe with all my heart that the arms and hearts of mothers that have ached for their lost children will have the opportunity of hugging them, and the father's hand, which never held the little hand, will be given the privilege."[4]

Barb took a deep breath and blew her nose. After wiping her tears, she reached out and took my hand, eyes still on our dinner guests. "Bill, I can't tell you how much this means to me—to us! Thank you so much."

"You're welcome. But most of all, we follow and serve a great God. One who loves little children and us more than we can imagine."

Barb and I were so relieved to understand that we will see and meet the four children we never saw. We'll hold them close and hug them tight. They could be babies or they could be as big as NFL linemen, but they will be there waiting for us. For years, we have remembered them by honoring them on the anniversary of the days they entered heaven—January 29, February 18, May 8, and August 2.

For some time, we weren't sure why God allowed the tumult and turmoil of four miscarriages. But we also knew that on this side of heaven, most of our "why" questions don't have answers, that God's ways do not always make sense. That said, we had reached a place where we were at peace because, in his mercy, God showed us a few of the reasons for the storms he either allowed or caused.

Most notably, he used them to draw our family and us closer to each other and closer to him. Seeing the ultrasounds and feeling the quickening of each unborn child persuaded us of the sanctity and inestimable value of life from the moment of conception.

In addition, Barb and I now understood the terrible pain both the mother and father experience with the loss of an unborn baby in a way that those who have not walked this path cannot. We could now sympathize and cry with other couples and be transmitters of comfort and consolation to couples on this sad path.

We became convinced that the millstones of tragedies that had hung around each of our necks would be transformed into stepping-stones of joy. For us, the full measure of healing comfort that was coming would be a precious gift that would give us much peace and confidence in the future.

However, our community would soon face a storm of inconceivable size and destruction that would shake our peace and confidence. It was time to batten down the hatches in more ways than one as an onrushing and terrible tornado took direct aim at a young physician, his wife, and their community.

34

Tempest and Terror

ONE FEBRUARY WEEKEND, our kids were away and John was on call for our practice. Sunday afternoon, I grilled for Barb, and we enjoyed a quiet evening and yet another glorious sunset across Lake Toho before turning in early.

A powerful thunderstorm awakened me just before midnight. It wasn't the wind or the relentless sheets of rain that roused me; it was the flashing of lightning bolts occurring every few seconds and the constant roll of thunderclaps vibrating our windows.

I got up, put on my robe and slippers, and walked to our bedroom window. The lightning illuminated the night sky almost without a break. The reverberations from the thunder continued to intensify as our windows rattled and our home quivered. *It's getting closer and closer*, I thought.

A blinding flash of lightning struck the transformer in front of our house. It exploded in flames, smoke, and green sparks, like a giant firecracker, causing me to jump back. Instantly, our electricity went out. If that wasn't frightening enough, I noticed a bright neon purplish hue outside our window. I had never seen anything like it. I stared out as the fluorescence slowly diminished, noting that the rain and lightning had suddenly stopped as if the explosion was either an exclamation mark at the end of the storm or a prelude for something worse to come.

A dull rumble enveloped our home and grew in force. I assumed it was another arm of the storm blowing in from across the lake, so I walked to the back of our house to see if I could get a glimpse of the wall of rain should lightning illumine it. Hail began a deafening *rat-tat-tat* against the roof, windows, and back deck. *Holy Moly!* I thought as the hail grew larger—going from dime-size to the size of golf and tennis balls.

The ground trembled as the sound strengthened and deepened. It was like a freight train was racing toward our back deck. It was pitch-dark, and I leaned toward the bank of our back windows as the sound became even more ferocious. The windows flexed in and out as a wall of water hit our roof and windows with such force the house shuddered. There was so much water rushing off the roof that it looked like I was standing behind a waterfall!

"Get away from the windows!" Barb yelled as she ran up behind me and jerked me back. The noise, wind, and rain were unbearable—far worse than any hurricane we experienced as kids in Louisiana. "The windows are going to break!" she screamed.

My mind raced. *What's the safest room?* I couldn't think of a place in the house that didn't have windows—even our bathroom. *Hold on!* I thought. *The kids' bathroom! It doesn't have a window.* I grabbed Barb. "Let's go!"

"Wait!" she cried, looking outside. "I think it's over."

She was right. Although the water was still rushing in torrents off the roof, the sound and fury of the wind had ceased. A blanket of silence wrapped our home. "I'll get a flashlight!" Barb said. As she was retrieving it, I stepped through our back door. Only a drizzle was falling.

She handed me the flashlight, and I swept the bright beam around, illuminating our back deck. A thick layer of branches and debris covered it. A huge limb from one of the oak trees was resting on the roof of our family room. As I turned to walk toward it, I almost slipped on a slimy object on the deck. I bent over to pick it up, and to my shock, it was a small plastic package of hamburger meat.

"Look at the label," Barb said. "It's from Winn-Dixie."

"The only one in town is across the lake. It must be five miles from here."

Barb nodded. "Let's check the front of the house."

We went through our home to the front porch and gasped as the flashlight beam exposed a lagoon of water and floating debris in our front yard. "Our porch is at least two feet off the ground," I said. "This is an absolute lake. Thank the Lord, our house is as high as it is. The storm must have picked up part of the lake and dumped it on our house and yard. No wonder so much water was coming off the roof!" I flashed the light across our new pond to the front yard beyond. My jaw dropped at the sight of mounds of strewn debris and branches as far as I could see.

"I guess we should try to get some sleep. Come dawn, we can survey the damage better."

Barb pulled me close. "First, how about a prayer of thanks for our safety and the protection of our home?"

It delighted me to do so, although at that moment, I had no idea how close we had come to our own indescribable calamity.

35

Night of Tornadoes

Before first light, our landline's shrill ring roused me. The electricity was still off.

"Walt, this is John. Are you and Barb okay?"

"We are. Heck of a windstorm, thunderstorm, or squall we had, wasn't it?" I said.

"You haven't heard?"

"What?"

"It wasn't any of those, Walt. They say it was an F4 tornado. It's devastated Osceola County. The edge passed within one hundred yards of your house and almost hit Bill and Polly's house. Winds were over two hundred and fifty miles per hour. It's destroyed countless homes and buildings. The weather guys say that the early indications are that it was really fast moving, a couple of hundred yards wide, and may have been on the ground fifteen miles or so. The TV images are devastating. Many have died, and they report scores missing. Hundreds, maybe thousands, injured. Many are critical."

I felt the blood drain from my face. "Oh my goodness!"

"Pete Gonzales called me to the hospital not too long ago. As the news came in, we began setting up a mass casualty triage. I ran over to check the office. We have no damage, and our electricity is working. So I've volunteered for us to help. Our office will be one of several locations taking in and triaging those with minor injuries. We sure could use help. Can you come?"

"Absolutely! When?"

"As soon as you can get there. I'll call Susan and have her get Judy, Jean, Jackie, and as many of our staff there as soon as possible. See ya there. Gotta go!" He hung up.

Barb slept as I pulled on scrubs, left her a note, pulled out a light coat, and stepped outside into the first light of a very cool dawn. Our front yard lagoon had receded, leaving a thick layer of branches, trash, and other debris strewn across the lawn. The carport, which did not appear damaged, had protected Barb's car and my old truck, but an overpowering fragrance of citrus wafted around me—several of our fruit trees had been shredded, leaving crushed grapefruit and oranges scattered across the yard.

The driveway was passable, and the road to the office was away from the storm's path. I made it to the practice and joined John and our staff as they streamed in, preparing to receive injuries. We all arrived within minutes of each other.

"Everyone's accounted for," Susan said, "except Nicole." Susan's eyes misted, and her lips trembled. Nicole was an older woman who often volunteered at our office. "Her house is in a neighborhood destroyed by the twister. Search and rescue is going house-to-house."

We all stopped, and John led a prayer for Nicole and all the families affected by the storm, as well as for wisdom and guidance for us. We did not know how many might come, but we feared and prepared for the worst.

Susan, Jean, and Jackie began making temporary charts for folks we'd be seeing who were not our patients. They also called our patients to reschedule their appointments and invited several lay ministers to volunteer in our waiting room to assist the injured as they arrived.

In the clinical area, Judy, the other nurses, and our back-office staff joined John and me as we began pulling out supplies to clean and dress wounds, take X-rays, sew up lacerations, set and cast fractures, give tetanus and antibiotic shots, and dispense any medications we could. In the background, a radio newscaster reported:

> Outsiders consider hurricanes to be the most significant environmental risk for Floridians. Since written records have been kept, approximately five hundred of these storms have hit Florida—more than any other state, with an average of about three a year. When it comes to hurricanes, weather experts consider Kissimmee one of Florida's safest cities because of our inland location. The same is not true for our tropical monsoons. We are known as "the thunderstorm capital of the US." As a result, lightning is the state's leading cause of weather-related deaths. In fact, we're number one in the US for deaths by lightning.
>
> However, more fearful than these are the tornadoes that roar across our fair state where they kill four times as many folks per year as hurricanes. In fact, on a per-mile basis, Florida leads the country in the highest number of tornadoes and tornado-related deaths—experiencing more killer tornadoes than the infamous "Tornado Alley" of the Great Plains. Ours stay on the ground longer, are harder to see coming, more likely to drop from the heavens during the cold season, and much more frequent at nighttime—all of which increase their capacity to maim, mutilate, or kill unsuspecting quarry as happened in Osceola County last night.

"Did anybody know all that?" John asked no one in particular as he worked. Heads shook all around. Several Red Cross volunteers arrived with a trailer to set up a relief station in our parking lot and prepared to hand out coffee, hot chocolate, doughnuts, and blankets to those needing them. As they stocked our waiting room with food and drink, they told us that a contingent of Red Cross personnel would soon arrive at the hospital with several large trailers for showers, food and clothing, and emergency communications for contacting next of kin and other critical needs.

The volunteers also informed us the city was turning the downtown Civic Center into an emergency shelter. The county planned to set up tents on the Silver Spurs rodeo grounds to receive others who were hurt or homeless.

As we waited for our first patients to arrive, we shared coffee and doughnuts and watched the horror stories playing out on the waiting room television. One emergency official said it was the deadliest tornado event in Florida history. John turned up the volume.

"It's being called the 'Night of Tornadoes,' with at least twelve confirmed funnel clouds touching down in a massive swath of destruction and devastation from Kissimmee to Daytona Beach," the news anchor reported. "Early reports indicate over twenty confirmed fatalities along at least a thirty-mile track of carnage. Cars have been sucked off the Florida Turnpike and dumped hundreds of yards from the road. Scores are severely to critically injured, and as a result, hospital emergency rooms are now disaster centers. We're receiving early estimates that thousands of homes and buildings have been destroyed or damaged."

The TV weatherman added, "Many of the storms registered at least F3 on the Fujita scale, meaning the winds clocked at 158 to 206 miles per hour. However, the deadliest was the F4 tornado that struck Osceola County with up to 260-mile-per-hour winds. An F5 has wind speeds of 261 miles an hour or more. The damage must be awful. We have a team trying to make it down there and will bring more details as they come available."

We watched an interview with Dr. Shashi Gore, the Orange-Osceola County medical examiner, that shocked us: "The most common cause of death appears to be blunt-force trauma," he began. "For some, it was the equivalent of falling from a plane. Some bodies had been carried more than a quarter of a mile. We already have twenty-two bodies from Osceola County. It appears the hardest hit."[1]

When asked when he might release the identities of the deceased, the doctor explained, "The injuries may make it very difficult to identify many of the victims. A temporary delay is expected when death involves such massive natural forces as a tornado. The force is tremendous. A 260-mile-an-hour wind is equivalent to the speed a jet reaches at the end of a runway when taking off. Think of objects going that fast hitting a person."

A reporter interviewed Kissimmee Mayor Attkisson. "I'm announcing a dusk-to-dawn curfew in all damaged areas, which involves a significant part of our county, to guard against looting." He added, "I want to warn building contractors and handymen that they will *not* be allowed to take advantage of victims. We will *not* tolerate that. Our message is treat our people with utmost respect or face the full impact of the law."

He then announced the triage centers. "For those from the north and east part of our city, go to Drs. Hartman and Larimore's office on East Oak Street. The Red Cross and medical care are available at no cost."

We had no idea what the day was about to bring.[2]

36

Haunting Silence

CARS BEGAN PULLING UP and the injured unloaded. "Time to go to work!" John exclaimed. My first set of patients all came from one family that lived in a neighborhood close to our home.

"The storm woke us as it began to tear our house apart," the father, Greg, explained. "Our bedroom wall just blew out into the yard. I grabbed my wife, tucked her in a bathroom at the house's center, and ran to my girls' bedroom. I grabbed them as the storm pulled our roof off."

"We could feel the wind trying to suck us out," the oldest girl said, beginning to cry. Her mother held her close. "It was hard to walk, the wind was so strong. But we all made it to the bathroom."

The mother, Kelly, recounted even more details. "We were in total blackness alternating with blinding bursts of lightning. Because we had no roof, the bathroom would light up with each bolt. The air was a thick cloud of sheetrock and insulation. Wreckage and debris flew everywhere. The girls screamed and cried in terror. We just huddled down in the tub, and Greg pulled the shower curtain over us."

"Sheets of rain pelted us," the youngest daughter explained.

"Then our puppy ran into the bathroom and jumped into the tub with us. We barely had room to breathe."

"The lightning reminded me of a strobe light," Greg added. "Bathroom tiles shattered and flew around. I think the shards caused a lot of our cuts."

"Then it ended—just as suddenly as it started," the middle child said.

"We just hugged and cried." Kelly pulled her daughters close. "We were so glad to be alive. Our entire home—gone! Nothing left but the bathroom. One of my girls suggested we sing a hymn."

The girls, for the first time, smiled and giggled.

"What?" I asked, wondering what they found so funny.

"None of us could remember the words to a *single* hymn," the middle girl explained. "So Daddy led us in singing 'Kumbaya, My Lord.'"

Greg laughed. "I think it may have been the most grateful hymn ever offered to the Lord."

One girl had stepped on a nail, but it was a superficial wound. They all had cuts, but none required stitches. Another daughter had a sprained ankle; the third a sore neck and head from being hit by a flying piece of lumber. I X-rayed Greg's injured hand. He had no broken or dislocated bones. Judy and I cleaned and steri-stripped cuts, then washed and dressed their abrasions and superficial lacerations. Judy put a lace-up brace on the sprained ankle, while I fitted Greg with a hand and wrist brace.

"I located a flashlight after the storm passed," Greg told us. "Fortunately, it worked. It was still rainy and cold, but I needed to get my family to safety. Then I planned to return to help our neighbors—at least those still alive. As we walked out of the neighborhood to a friend's house in the next development, our neighborhood looked like a war zone," Greg explained. "All the houses were gone or, at least, mostly gone. Any left were heavily damaged."

"Except one house that stood with no more damage than a bent television antenna," Kelly added. "The houses on both sides of it looked like nothing but a pile of rubble—surreal. We passed one home that had only a chest of drawers standing there in the middle of the rubble. All the drawers were gone, but a TV was still on top of it. Another home had a little curio cabinet standing next to what was left of the living room. The cabinet was filled with trinkets. They all looked fine—no broken glass and not one object out of place. Another home had no garage, but the cars sat there with no obvious damage. The silence was haunting until we heard the strangest sound."

"A snow globe music box," one of the girls said. "I picked it up out of a yard. Do you know what it was playing?"

I shook my head.

"'Silent Night,'" she said, smiling as tears filled her eyes. "We remembered every verse. Even the third one." The girls looked at each other and then sang it a cappella and in harmony:

> Silent night, holy night, Son of God, love's pure light.
> Radiant beams from Thy holy face, with the dawn of
>   redeeming grace.
> Jesus, Lord at Thy birth, Jesus, Lord at Thy birth.[1]

It was a sacred moment and may have been the most beautiful and heartfelt version of "Silent Night" I had ever heard—at least, up to that moment.[2]

37

Almost Squashed

WAYNE AND JANET brought their two children in for minor physical trauma. In addition, both kids were traumatized by the tornado, and their parents wanted a prescription for Benadryl syrup in case they needed it to help the children sleep over the next few nights. As Judy was cleaning and dressing their wounds, they told me their story.

"You know, we had wild weather all week," Wayne began. "Then, just after midnight, I woke up to what sounded like a jet coming across the lake—you know, heading up to the Orlando airport—except much louder than usual. Honestly, it sounded like it was a hundred feet off the ground. I had never heard a tornado before, but at that moment, I was wide awake and knew *exactly* what it was. The noise was horrific and getting worse by the second. I screamed to wake up Janet so we could run to get the kids."

"Wayne scared me to death. He *never* screams," Janet added. "I yelled, 'You get John!' and I ran to the other end of the house to grab Lyndsey."

"When Mom woke me, she about jerked my arm off," Lyndsey said. "She yelled 'tornado' and pulled me toward the door. I started screaming at her that I needed to get Joshua."

"Joshua?" I asked. As far as I knew, there were only two children in the family.

"My guinea pig!" Lyndsey said. "I grabbed his cage, and me and Mommy ran into the hall and lay down. Joshua just lay down in his cage. The horrible noise was getting louder and louder."

"And the whole house was shaking like we were in an earthquake," Janet added.

"At that same moment," Wayne said, "I ran into John's room and grabbed him. I remember looking into the kids' shared bathroom. We had always told the kids that if there ever was a severe storm, they should run into their bathroom and get into the tub. We always felt it was the safest room because there were no windows. But for some reason, I ran past it into the hallway, put John next to Lyndsey and Janet, and lay across the three of them."

Lyndsey smiled. "Daddy's big enough to cover us three."

"But he was *so* brave!" John exclaimed, looking at his daddy with evident pride.

Janet's voice was tremulous as she shook her head, trying to gather her thoughts. "And I don't know why, but I had this sudden, horrifying sense that the house was going to explode apart somehow. It was overwhelming." She shook and began to cry. Wayne held her close.

"The sound of the proverbial freight train was getting louder and louder, and all the windows blew out."

"Then *it* happened," Janet whispered.

"What?" Judy asked.

"It was like a massive explosion," Wayne answered. "The entire house shook like it would come off the foundation—like in a horror movie."

"Almost in slow motion," Janet said, trying to suppress her trembling.

"Then a giant, humongous, ginormous, colossal oak tree came crashing down on our house," John said. "It completely flattened my room *and* the bathroom. If we'd gone in that bathroom, we all would have been squashed like bugs!"

Lyndsey shook her head. "We would have been smashed flat."

"The attic fan above us had flipped upside down and was banging up and down, making a terrible racket," Wayne said. "I was scared to death it was going to fall on top of us and slice up my back. In that type of moment, you don't know if you're going to live or not. Be killed by the house collapsing. Be electrocuted." He grimaced. "You know what's happening is bad, but you don't know how bad. Glass was flying everywhere. Walls were shaking and cracking. Wood beams were splintering. We stayed huddled in the hallway—it seemed like an hour. Then, as suddenly as it started, it was over. The morning news said it only lasted seventeen seconds."

"To me, it seemed like an entire day," John said.

"A lifetime to me," Janet added in a whisper, both of her hands shaking.

Wayne continued their story. "Then it was over. I got up and found a flashlight. It was surreal. We had Precious Moments figurines on a shelf at the end of the hall—some were smashed to smithereens, and some survived untouched."

"In the kitchen," Janet added, "a jar of tomatoes exploded and left a perfect circle of sauce. Other jars and canisters hadn't moved an inch!"

"And," John pointed out, "water was coming in through the roof and every light fixture."

"Our house was trashed," Janet said. "The burst windows and crushed roof let in lake water, leaves, and trash. And outside, oh my, it looked like a war zone."

"What did you all do?" Judy asked. "You must have been wet and cold."

"Soaked to the bone!" John declared.

"We took the kids over to Dick and Kay Simmons's house—Janet's aunt and uncle—located in the next neighborhood," Wayne said. "I found a dry quilt to throw on the kids and Janet grabbed Lyndsey's Easter dress, which we had just purchased. It was hanging on the bathroom door like nothing happened."

"And, of course, we brought Joshua with us!" Lyndsey added.

"At dawn, I went back to look at the house," Wayne said. "It was crazy. We lost three massive oak trees and a huge magnolia tree—completely uprooted and gone. Who knows where? All the shingles had been ripped off the house. The roof had completely separated from the top of the sides of the house. Who knows what held it on? Pine straw, leaves, and trash were plastered on the stucco. And that oak tree that blew over and crushed John's bedroom and the kids' bath—it was at least fifty feet of limbs and trunk that crushed the house. Even the lower limbs of the tree were about two feet across, and the trunk was massive—at least three to four feet across. My car, a big, heavy Mercury Grand Marquis, looked like it had been spun like a doughnut, leaving circular tire marks in the mud, and then slammed down parallel to the house instead of perpendicular. Then I saw it—painted on the house."

He was quiet for a moment, and Janet took his hand.

"There was spray-paint on the front of our house," Janet said.

"Why?" I asked.

"Apparently, search and rescue had combed our home and then sprayed a large *X*," Wayne said. "It showed that they had completed their search. The date and time were spray-painted above the *X*—'2-23-0400'—for February 23rd at 4:00 a.m. The search team had painted 'Cas01' to the left side of the *X*—I assume for Casualty Team #1. To the right of the *X*, it said, 'None,' which meant there were no hazards inside. Then, below the *X*, the team had painted the number four and just below that the number zero."

Wayne stopped, and his lips trembled. Janet took his hand.

"What did that mean?" I asked.

"Four survivors—no corpses found," Janet said.

Lyndsey added, "It was a miracle, Dr. Walt. A genuine miracle."

All four of them nodded.

38

A True Miracle

LATE THAT MORNING, Abby arrived with her two children, Eva and James, her baby brother. Although covered with a warm blanket, Abby was wet, shaking, and alternating between sobbing and hyperventilating. I gave her a shot of an antianxiety medication.

"What happened?" I asked as Abby calmed down some and Judy began taking the vital signs of the whole family. At first glance, they all seemed physically healthy except for the scratches, bruises, and abrasions that so many storm victims had.

"We went to bed early," Abby told us. "Eva wanted to sleep with me, which was fine since my husband is off on a business trip. I put little James in a bassinet by the bed. But I woke up when the tornado hit. It turns out it went right over the house. It happened so fast. The house shook, and the roof blew off. Eva began screaming."

"It was *very* scary!" Eva added, sounding calm and grown-up.

"What happened?" I asked.

"I grabbed Eva, and we rolled onto the floor between the wall and the bed next to the bassinet. It was dark; but somehow I could see the bedroom windows blowing out as the walls began to disintegrate. Debris swirled all around. I reached up to grab James as his cradle and the mattress began to be sucked away. I was able to grab his little hand as the storm tried to suck him out." Abby broke down sobbing.

Judy sat down by Abby, put her arm around her, and held her close.

I handed Abby a box of tissues. She dabbed her eyes and blew her nose, although her tears continued to flow. "I tried to pull him toward me while the storm was pulling him away. I wanted to get him by Eva and me, and then I was going to pull the mattress over us. But the force was too strong. Before I knew it, the storm sucked James and the mattress away, and he disappeared. I remember screaming. Then nothing."

She dissolved into more tears.

"Me and Mommy rolled under the bed, Dr. Walt," Eva said. "Mommy was asleep, and I just held her close. She wouldn't wake up, so I held her to keep her warm and said my prayers. When we woke up, we were trapped under the bed. The rescue squad found us. The Lord answered my prayers, Dr. Walt. They saved us."

"I can't even imagine how scary that must have been, Eva," I said. "You are one very courageous and brave young woman."

She smiled and said, very matter-of-factly, "I am!"

Abby regained her composure and continued with her story. "I don't remember anything else until they were digging us out," she said. "Apparently, part of a bedroom wall and the ceiling had fallen on the box spring, trapping us. Fortunately, the debris created a warm, dry, and protective shelter. Believe it or not, we must have fallen asleep for a bit."

I looked down at little James, fast asleep in his mother's arms, then into Abby's tearful eyes.

"I woke up when I heard noises. A fireman found us," Abby said. "I panicked and screamed to him that they had to find little James. He tried to calm me down, but I couldn't stop the panicked feelings. They were overwhelming me." Abby collapsed into Judy's arms.

Eva patted her mother's arm and explained. "They took Mommy and me to the fire truck and covered us with warm blankets and gave us some hot chocolate. They told us they would look for my brother."

"I knew they'd never find him," Abby said. "But Eva held my hand and prayed that they would. She *knew* Jesus was going to answer another prayer. She *knew* it! And just then, another firefighter came running up. 'I found him! I found him!' he kept yelling. He ran up and put baby James in my arms then said, 'He's cold, but not even scratched.' I looked him over. He was right. He was wet, cold, and shivering, but he smiled. I held him close and couldn't stop crying. He was gone—good as gone—forever. Then found—found safe and sound."

"I knew he was okay," Eva added.

"Where'd they find him?" Judy asked.

"The firefighter told me that during his search, he found a mattress sitting about six feet off the ground. It was stuck in an oak tree that had blown over. He saw a baby's leg sticking over the edge of the mattress. It didn't move, and he suspected the worst. He reached up and grabbed it. The leg jerked, and the baby cried. It scared him to death, but he had found *our* James!"

Eva looked up at me and added, very seriously, "Now, Dr. Walt, that's not only an answer to prayer, *that* is a true miracle."

I smiled and nodded in agreement, as I had seen many a prayer answered that were uttered from a child's lips. I've heard it said, "One of the most powerful forces on earth is the prayer of a child"[1]—or for us older folks, a childlike prayer.

We worked through the day, seeing over one hundred patients in the clinic. As supplies would run low, the hospital or Red Cross would replace them. Many volunteers had joined the effort, and things went well. After saying a prayer with the last family I examined that day, I left the exam room to find Judy waiting in the hall.

"Ready for one more miracle?" she asked, her countenance beaming. "Dr. Hartman is checking them now."

I followed her to one of John's exam rooms and entered to find our volunteer, Nicole, and her two grandchildren. She stood to give me a tearful hug.

"Looks like all the injuries are minor," John commented, jotting down some last notes. "Scratches and bruises to the body, the soul, and the spirit."

"What happened?" It seemed to be the question I asked most that day. "Are you all right?"

"You won't believe *this* story," Judy interjected.

Nicole smiled and nodded. "That's right! When the storm hit, I gathered the grandchildren with me in a bathroom in the middle of the house. We heard our house being destroyed—like being blown up all around us. The walls wobbled. The floor trembled like a terrible earthquake or something. But the roof and walls of the bathroom held. When the tornado passed, we were all okay, but at first, the door wouldn't open. My grandson was able to force it open. I had a little battery-powered makeup light and shined it around.

"You will not believe this," the grandson said.

"Tell him!" Judy cajoled.

Nicole nodded at her grandson.

"I couldn't believe my eyes!" he began. "It was like we were in our attic."

"What?" I asked.

"It took me a minute to realize what happened," Nicole recounted. "All the walls had blown away, and our entire roof crashed down and covered us." She shuddered. "All of the roof eaves were on the ground. And since we had no dormers, there was no way out. Fortunately, we had water and were warm, so we waited."

Nicole sniffled and blew her nose. "Thank God there was no gas leak or fire," she added. "We would not have gotten out."

I asked my usual "So what happened?"

"We prayed, sang some songs, played a few mental games, and talked," Nicole said.

"It was like a campout or something," the granddaughter added.

"But with no s'mores," her brother said.

"Then we heard someone knocking on the roof," Nicole said. "They were the answer to our prayers. We started yelling and screaming and thumping back. Someone yelled for us to back away—that they would cut us out. A chainsaw started, and in a few minutes, we had a wide-open exit and walked out—right through the roof." She stopped to take a deep breath and blow her nose again.

"Then we looked around in shock. Our entire neighborhood—gone. No homes, no mailboxes, no trees. Debris and overturned cars and trucks in every direction as far as you could see."

She looked back. "God saved us. It was a miracle."

I could not disagree.

On the way home that evening, since crews had partially cleared Neptune Road, I was able to weave through the damage to Bill and Jane's driveway. When I parked, I saw Bill inspecting his backyard.

"Are you and Jane okay?" I asked as I walked up.

"We're blessed, Walt. No damage to our home or vehicles. It looks like we were just on the edge of the funnel. I heard you were on the other edge."

"Yup. It appears to have passed right between us."

"Lookie there!" He pointed across his farm fields. The funnel's path, etched into the earth, had covered his fields with a carpet of rubble. "I walked it off. Nearly three hundred yards wide. Trash of every imaginable sort. Contents from stores and houses, pictures and possessions, trees and boats, lumber and roofs. Some intact, most shredded. Since it was nearly an F5, some folks are calling it the 'Finger of God,' but not me. I believe he's got the whole

229

world in his hand. And if we have faith in him, he'll help us re-store all this carnage. I believe many miracles will come from this. I do."

"I've already seen a bunch, Bill. And like you, I believe more will come!"

39

Not Our
Final Home

THE REST OF THE WEEK, the weather remained clear, cloudless, and warm. Teams from as far away as the Midwest and Northeast helped Florida-based crews clear the roads and restore utilities. We discharged those admitted to the hospital, and the Red Cross found housing for the homeless. Clearing and rebuilding began. A team of volunteers from a church in North Georgia came to our neighborhood and spent two days trimming trees and hauling away debris from our and our neighbors' yards. They said they picked our house at random; however, I didn't believe there was anything accidental about it at all!

Officials confirmed seven severe tornadoes that struck between 10:55 p.m. and 2:30 a.m., resulting in 42 fatalities and at least 260 critical injuries. Four of the long-lived funnel clouds, on the ground from 8 to 38 miles, caused the most death and destruction—damaging 3,000 structures and destroying another 700.

The worst of the tornadoes was the one that hit us in Osceola County. When all was said and done, the official record declared it had been a severe F4 tornado—an apocalypse that traveled along the ground at an incredible 45 miles per hour, was on the ground 14 miles, and averaged a ground path of 250 yards wide.[1] Our community suffered 25 fatalities, 150 severe injuries, and over 1,000 damaged or destroyed structures. Not to mention that damage estimates topped fifty million dollars.

One factor that made these tornadoes so deadly was that they occurred overnight, when most residents slept. In those days, folks did not have a tone-alerted NOAA weather radio or smartphones to warn them of the impending danger. While officials had documented several outbreaks of strong and violent tornadoes in Central Florida over the preceding 120 years, the number of fatalities resulting from our storm was unprecedented—a historic event. But it could have been so much worse. The annual Silver Spurs Rodeo wrapped up that Sunday afternoon, and the eight thousand spectators and hundreds of participants cleared out just hours before the catastrophe. Spring training for baseball's Houston Astros was to begin that week. The thousands of expected fans were only one day from arriving.

Of all the memories I have from the destruction left behind, one stands out. The Saturday after the storm, our family walked over to Wayne and Janet's house to help them with cleanup. As we walked down Neptune Road, several of the massive power poles, broken ten to twenty feet off the ground, hung suspended from the thick power wires, swaying in the breeze.

Wayne showed me the oak tree trunk that had crushed John's bedroom and the kids' bathroom. It *was* massive. I could only mutter, "Amazing."

"Want to see something else astonishing?" Wayne asked. We walked around to the front of the house and looked at his large, solid wood door, which looked like the hide of a hedgehog or porcupine with countless half-inch- to one-inch-long pine needles impaled into it.

"Run your hand along them. They're stuck in deep. I guess that's what 250-mile-an-hour winds do with little projectiles."

I shook my head. "Guess you're glad you didn't open the front door."

"Don't even like to think about it," Wayne said.

He pointed to a house behind his. It was just a pile of rubble that literally looked like it had been bombed. "That's the house Abby and her husband owned." He pointed to another flattened oak tree. "That's the tree in which they found little James."

He looked away, as if in thought, and then turned back to me. "Walt, I know your faith is important to you. I was wondering something. How does God fit into this picture? If he's a loving, merciful God, why does he allow so much death and destruction? How does he choose to let little John live and so many others die?"

I was touched Wayne trusted me enough to ask such a difficult question. I thought for a minute about the fact that not all see an open door like this as a sacred opportunity to steward. Instead, it seemed to me, many try to kick the door open with some pat answer or Bible verse. With that in mind, I said a quick prayer to ask for wisdom.

"Wayne," I began, "that's a great question. No thinking person wouldn't ask the same thing. Barb and I taught our kids when they were young to pray before mealtimes, saying, 'God is great, God is good, let us thank him for our food.'

"But when you see the almost indiscriminate death and destruction we've seen this week, it's only natural to wonder, Is God great? Is God good? I mean, if he is all-powerful, could he not have prevented this disaster? And if he's truly good, why didn't he? Is that what you're thinking?"

Wayne nodded.

I sighed deeply. "I don't know that I have all the answers. In fact, I'm sure I don't. I believe God *is* great and God *is* good—that he is fair and just and loving—and this horrible event has not changed that. As a Christian, I'm called to worship the God of the storm before, during, and after it, and to look for and watch out for how he's at work during horrible events.

"I believe nothing happens in my life that God has not planned or permitted," I went on. "In trusting that he is sovereign in his greatness and goodness, I can trust him and have peace during a storm. Troubles, trials, and torments will still occur; death, destruction, and disability won't diminish; loss and life may not be restored; but the power of these things to defeat us is broken if we can trust that God is in fact in control and has a plan to bring good from the bad."

I could see Wayne was thinking and didn't have a question, so I continued, "To me, it's a mistake to think that God had nothing to do with the storm, but it's also a terrible mistake for us to act like we know exactly what God was doing and what he's going to do. When Job was in the midst of terrible circumstances, he and God had a discussion. Toward the end of it, Job admitted to God, 'I know that you can do anything, and no one can stop you. You asked, "Who is this that questions my wisdom with such ignorance?" It is I—and I was talking about things I knew nothing about, things far too wonderful for me.'"[2]

Wayne pointed at a bench on their front porch, and we sat. "So," he asked, "you don't think this tornado was just some blind quirk of nature? Some sort of accident? Some fickle weather event that blew my house apart and could have killed Janet or me or our kids, yet left this bench untouched?"

I shook my head. "I don't. In some way that I can't fully understand, God allows bad things and even bad people to exist, to happen, to destroy, for his purpose and our good. These types of events remind me of attributes of God, like his power or his holiness."

Wayne threw his arm up and out. "How can you look at this neighborhood, which looks like an atomic bomb went off, and say something like that?"

I knew he wasn't attacking me and was grateful he trusted me enough to ask about very difficult and heartfelt issues. "Another great question, Wayne. Again, I don't have all the answers, and I certainly don't fully understand untimely death and unmitigated disasters. But, at least for me, I've been able to thank God that, during and after this storm, he revealed himself to me and many of my patients in ways that we would never have known about or seen otherwise. That's what I've been praying this week: 'God, what are you trying to teach me, my staff and patients, and my friends about yourself?' I've seen mercy and compassion I would not have seen apart from the suffering that has occurred. I've seen the grace of God because of the existence of this terrible event."

"Because of or in the midst of?" Wayne asked.

"I think both, my friend." I was quiet a moment as I gathered my thoughts. "I see disease and disasters as God's invitation to wake up and realize what's really important in life—not our physical condition or our possessions but our spiritual condition." I turned to look Wayne in the eye. "Have you heard of C. S. Lewis?"

Wayne shook his head.

"He was a brilliant British professor who held positions in English literature at Oxford University and then was chair of medieval and renaissance literature at Cambridge University. To me, he's one of the intellectual giants of the twentieth century and one of the most influential writers of his day. Anyway, he wrote something like this: 'God whispers to us in our pleasures, speaks in our conscience, but shouts in our pain—it is his megaphone to rouse a deaf world.'[3] In other words, I think God sometimes allows disease, disorder, and disaster to get our attention and then to direct us into a closer personal relationship with himself."

Wayne's eyes misted, and he looked down.

His silence gave me the freedom to continue. "Our heavenly Father knows our most profound need is to be made right with him so that we can avoid the greatest of all potential disasters—going into eternity without him."

Wayne rubbed his chin. "So are you saying God can use the 'Finger of God' to direct us to the hand of God?"

"I like that, Wayne. Bill Judge once told me, 'God deals with us as gently as he can or as harshly as he must.'"

Wayne seemed to consider my comment. He furrowed his brow and looked back at me. "I can imagine that, as a doctor, you care for many, many patients as they walk in and through some pretty difficult storms in their lives."

"That's true. And to me, it seems that God often uses calamity to shake us awake and cause us to consider questions like, What's really important? What should I be giving my life to? Why am I working so hard to gain things that God says are only temporary?

"These events often allow people to begin to hear God's voice by slowing down and sometimes, for the first time in their lives, begin seeking him and his kingdom."

Wayne chuckled. "Seems like most of my friends put their hope in houses, cars, jobs, financial security. They put their trust not in God, but in people, power, pleasure, prestige, position, or possessions."

"I think that's true," I said, "at least until some disaster or disease shows up unexpectedly and jerks all those things away. These things can become a wake-up call—a reminder that the only proper place, the only safe place, the only eternally secure location for our hope and our future is in God and in him alone. Someone once said, 'You will never know God is all you need until God is all you have.' He reveals himself to people who seek and trust him—who stop pursuing the God they want and surrender to the God who is."

Wayne took in a deep breath and slowly released it. "Wow, I can tell you've thought a lot about these things."

"I have. As you said, every day I see people who are facing disease, a health disaster, a medical disorder, and even death sentences. I do all I can to heal them, but when I can't do that, I try to bring at least help and hope—true and lasting confidence and comfort that can only be found in God. I want them to come to understand that they can trust their unknown future to a known God. And the reason I can do that is because of what God promises to bring out of our sufferings.

"The Bible says that 'God is always at work for the good of

everyone who loves him'—the ones he has chosen for his purpose.[4] Wayne, I believe from the bottom of my heart that God is great and that God is good, and he's always at work on our behalf for our benefit and his glory, through thick and thin."

Wayne still seemed deep in thought.

"I have one last thought to share, if that's okay," I said.

He smiled and nodded.

"I'm not preaching too much, am I?"

Wayne laughed. "Well, you *are* preaching a lot. But this is *very* helpful for me!"

I nodded then said, "I've learned that in difficulties and disasters, calamities and catastrophe, God is saying, 'Look for me. Watch for me now but know that I don't intend for you to go through these things forever on earth—it's not your final home.' Jesus has promised that he will return to earth one day to make everything new again and live with his people. He promises an end to death, mourning, crying, and pain."[5]

Wayne nodded as tears streaked down his cheeks.

"As followers of Jesus, no matter how much we suffer, how much we hurt, we know we have something to look forward to! Bill Judge has taught me that when my life is rooted in God's will-be's instead of my were's or was'es, then I'll always experience eventual victory. In other words, God assures us, if we love him, what will be is ultimately and eternally more important than what has been or what is. Make sense?"

Wayne sniffled and wiped his tears, and then he embraced me in a bear hug. "It does," he whispered. "And it gives me great hope."

"Me too," I whispered back.

Wayne sat back and looked across the destruction surrounding us. "I think my family's future, like most people around here, will be forever changed by this storm." He bobbed his head. "This house belonged to Janet's grandparents. Over the last year, I've begun to sense a call to go into the ministry. We've, of course, talked a lot about that. But Janet wasn't sure—not with us having two children and good jobs. Most of all, Janet didn't want to leave the family home. But just this morning, she told me, 'Honey, you don't know what you can deal with until it happens. Maybe it's time to start thinking about seminary.' I kind of wondered if she still might be in shock. I guess time will tell. I sense that this is not our final home either."

40

Fear Not

THE DECEMBER AFTER the tornadoes hit our community, several area churches joined to commemorate Christmas with a unique memorial service at the Kissimmee Civic Center. The program was designed to remember those lost and celebrate our ongoing healing and recovery as families and a community. Our office staff attended together.

As we were finding our seats, we saw many familiar faces: Coach Baker and Kathy sitting with Connie Partin, as well as the Prathers, Sabettos, Judges, Rinkuses, Shearers, and many other patients and friends. Chief Frank Ross was there with his family and several officers, including Gib Michaels. Drs. Byerly, Sessions, and Gonzales all waved at us, although Dr. Gonzales looked bored—likely because he was not in the operating room.

Mayor Frank Attkisson began the service by welcoming the community. "Welcome, everyone. Christmas is a time each year for us to reflect and remember our losses, but it's also a magical time to heal and to celebrate together what we cherish the most: our faith, our family, and our friends. This Christmas has the potential to be one of our most memorable in a long time—not just because of the horrors this year brought but also because of the chance for new growth and new beginnings from the rich soil of difficult trials. I'd like to call up Pastor Tim Wilder to give our opening prayer."

Tim walked to the podium. "The Lord invites each of us to turn to him in our times of great distress, disillusionment, and disappointment. Let's do so this evening. Will you pray with me?"

Everyone bowed their heads.

"Almighty God, we ask that you continue to heal our traumatized souls hearts and crushed spirits. Continue to remove the heaviness from our hearts and give us the strength to live full, meaningful, and abundant lives. Help us release the past and continue forward, growing in you and reflecting upon you, your Word, and your love. Lord, help us be still and remember that you are God. Thank you for loving us, caring for us, healing us, and promising us eternal life. Thank you for the Word of God to guide and comfort us. Thank you for your Spirit, who can provide us love, joy, peace, patience, kindness, goodness, faithfulness, gentleness, and self-control. Thank you for the people of God with whom we can journey, serve, and love in life together. In Jesus's name, we all pray. Amen!" Tim looked up to the people gathered at the center. "And now, Dr. John Hartman has a reading for us, and he'll be followed by a short message from Pastor Pete."

John stood, walked up to the podium, and read the Christmas story from Luke's Gospel to the hushed crowd.[1]

After he sat, Pastor Pete rose to speak. "It's humbling for those of us who preach every week to realize that the most powerful pulpit isn't a pulpit at all," he began. "And often, the most effective preacher isn't actually a preacher. Listening to Dr. John read this beautiful gospel story once again, I marvel at its power. What is it about Luke's sharing of the simple nativity story that makes it so enduring and endearing year after year, century after century? I wonder if it's not the phrase right there in the middle of the story, 'Do not be afraid.'[2]

"And then it gets better," Pastor Pete went on. "'Behold, I bring you good news of great joy which will be for all the people; for today in the city of David there has been born for you a Savior, who is Christ the Lord.'[3] At this moment, the course of human history changed forever. God became one of us. 'History' was divided in two, BC and AD, and became 'his story.' The Savior's very name proclaims this miraculous truth: Emmanuel, God with us. And he has been with us even during this challenging year.

"The Christmas angels' words are for us also. 'Do not be afraid.' From over two thousand years ago, those words reach out to us with hope and consolation. No matter who you are, no matter where you live, no matter what your circumstances, *this* is what matters. You no longer have to fear—'Do not be afraid.'

"To those who lost someone you love in the tornado, to those still without homes or jobs, to the children and families pulled apart, the Christmas angel says, 'Do not be afraid.'

"To those still sick and suffering, those still lonely and lost, those still experiencing nightmares and traumatic stress—yes, even to those who feel that maybe God has forgotten you—the angel of the Lord, his messenger, says, 'Do not be afraid.'

"Why? Because as Luke tells us, even in the coldest and darkest of nights, there is light, help, and hope. A Savior has been born for you who is Christ the Lord, so 'Do not be afraid.' God came to us as a baby that we could not help but love, and he grew into a Savior we dare not *not* love because he loves each of us so much. So 'Do not be afraid!'

"In this Christmas season, the age-old story is, 'I proclaim to you good news of great joy that will be for all the people: . . . a Savior was born.'[4] Christmas is a reminder of God's overpowering love for us—his reassurance to our community is that he was, is, and will be with us, at all times, through all events, good and bad, big and small. He walks with us, he grieves with us, he comforts us, he hopes with us. Remember his name: Emmanuel, God with us. And 'Do not be afraid.'

"Now, enjoy with me a reenactment of that holy night."

After these words, the stage went black.[5]

41

The Best Gift

THE CURTAIN QUICKLY ROSE, revealing a life-size stable with cows, sheep, and a braying donkey—causing folks, especially the kids, to laugh.

The narrator began, "Christmas is the celebration of the Savior's birth, but it is also the story of a mother's love, fear, faith, and obedience. It tells of promises fulfilled, a cradle rocked, a journey both ending and beginning at the same time. It is the story of everything to be cherished in a world full of storms in which so much can be damaged or lost."

As the music to "Silent Night" began, I recognized Abby and her husband, dressed up as Mary and Joseph, kneeling in front of a small manger lined with straw. I looked in front of them, but the crib was empty. Three girls walked out, dressed as angels, singing:

> Silent night, holy night, all is calm, all is bright.
> 'Round yon Virgin Mother and Child, Holy Infant so
>   tender and mild.
> Sleep in heavenly peace, sleep in heavenly peace.[1]

Barb leaned over to me and whispered, "It's Greg and Kelly's girls."

Recalling the snow globe that they found the night of the tornado, I sensed my eyes misting as I remembered the first time I heard them sing that hymn. As they began the second verse, a fourth angel walked out from one side of the stage, carrying a baby. I recognized the angel as Sandi Lynch, cradling little James.

Wayne, Janet, and their kids, dressed up as shepherds, entered from the other side of the stage. Wayne had recently decided to go to seminary and enter the ministry. He wanted to go to a Kentucky seminary but had just learned the seminary was locating a branch in nearby Orlando. They were over the moon, delighted they would be in the inaugural class. As they crossed the stage, they were singing:

> Silent night, holy night! Shepherds quake at the sight!
> Glories stream from heaven afar.

The choir, all dressed as angels, brightly illuminated the stage as they walked up from the shadows in the back, singing:

> Heavenly hosts sing Alleluia!
> Christ, the Savior is born,
> Christ, the Savior is born!

Sandi knelt and gave James to Abby as tears streaked down both of their faces. Abby continued to weep as she placed little James, representing the baby Jesus, in the manger. The words to the next verse were projected on large screens on either side of the stage as the narrator said, "Would you join us in singing?" Without being told to, everyone stood and sang.

> Silent night, holy night, Son of God, love's pure light.
> Radiant beams from Thy holy face, with the dawn of
>   redeeming grace.
> Jesus, Lord at Thy birth, Jesus, Lord at Thy birth.

After the song had finished, Pastor Pete walked back to the podium and had everyone take their seats. He thanked everyone whose hard work made this special evening possible. "It is a great gift to understand that we do not travel alone in life but in the company of others—our families, our friends, and our faith communities," he said to the crowd. "During our storms of this year, so many offered a hand up and hands out to hold, hug, and help us.

"May this Christmas bring joy to each of our worlds because the Lord, the greatest gift of all, has come. May we each receive him as King, may each heart invite him in and prepare him a room. Let's pray."

We bowed our heads once again as Pastor Pete began.

"Lord, despite our many tears this year, you are still our source of love, joy, and peace. You are no longer a babe in the manger. You are Lord of Lords and King of Kings. May we celebrate you this Christmas, and as we approach this new year and the rest of our lives here on earth, may we all heed your call and command—'Do not be afraid'—for you are indeed with us at all times. In Jesus's name, Amen."

Pete looked into the crowd and said one last thing. "And now, would you join me in our final Christmas carol? Merry Christmas! May God bless us, every one!"

The music began and the words shone on the screen as we all sang:

> Joy to the world, the Lord is come!
> Let earth receive her King!
> Let every heart prepare Him room,
> And Heaven and nature sing.
> And Heaven and nature sing.
> And Heaven, and Heaven, and nature sing.[2]

I awoke early the next morning. Since I had no patients in the hospital, I had time for a cup of coffee at home and an extended quiet time to sit and ponder the festivities of the night before. Most poignant to me was the nativity scene, which embodied so much joy, so much thankfulness.

The entire evening represented a time of generosity, gratitude, and gentleness—a solemn event in which the citizens of our small town could close out the year as one now-interconnected family. An occasion among all the trees and ornaments, the glitter and decorations, the pageantry and singing, the prayers and words of comfort, in which one precious act shone brighter than the rest: the simple undertaking of sharing all we had gone through—the pain and the joy, the horror and the healing, the losses and the hope.

To me, this beautiful ceremony provided a great message of healing from the past and hope for the future, in which my family and my community could celebrate turning darkness to light. A time to replace emotional and spiritual scabs and scars with the refreshing salve of optimism and expectation. Our season of terrible storms was finally ending, replaced with the expectation of new and better seasons to come.

That Christmas I realized, more than ever before, not only that fortunate are those who find and feel love but also eternally well-off are those who experience and abide in love's true Author. He is the best of all gifts one can accept, experience, *and* share.

Epilogue

LATE ON CHRISTMAS EVE—after Barb, Kate, and Scott were in their beds—I sat in front of our beautifully decorated tree. A warm, crackling fire filled our wood-burning stove.

On the table by my chair sat an orchid, hybridized and given to our family by my friend Jimmy Sabetto. The tag at the base of the plant read "*Cattlianthe Kate Larimore.*" It was proudly displaying its first bloom after seven years of development.

This plant was a precious Christmas gift to our family that, for many years, whenever she bloomed, would remind us of our family's growth in the early years of my practice as a family physician.

In the card that accompanied it, Jimmy had written,

God chose to love me, Cynthia, and Gina through you and your family. I think his love sloshes out of you to everyone he brings into your life and your practice. Someone sent me this wonderful poem not too long ago. It's titled "The Vessel" and was written a few decades ago by a pastor's wife, Beulah V. Cornwall. It reminds me of you. Merry Christmas, my friend!

The Master was searching for a vessel to use;
on the shelf, there were many—which one would he
   choose?
"Take me," cried the gold one, "I'm shiny and bright;
I'm of great value, and I do things just right.
My beauty and luster will outshine the rest
and for Someone like You, Master, gold would be best!"

The Master passed on with no word at all;
He looked at the silver urn, narrow and tall.
"I'll serve You, dear Master; I'll pour out Your wine,
and I'll be at Your table whenever You dine.
My lines are so graceful, my carvings so true,
and silver will always compliment You."

Unheeding, the Master passed on to the brass.
It was wide-mouthed and shallow and polished like
   glass.
"Here! Here!" cried the vessel. "I know I will do.
Place me on Your table for all men to view."

"Look at me," called the goblet of crystal so clear.
"My transparency shows my contents so dear.
Though fragile am I, I will serve You with pride,
and I'm sure I'll be happy in Your house to abide."

The Master came next to a vessel of wood.
Polished and carved, it solidly stood.
"You may use me, dear Master," the wooden bowl said,
"but I'd rather You used me for fruit—please, no bread!"

Then the Master looked down and saw a vessel of clay—
empty and broken, it helplessly lay.
No hope had that vessel that the Master might choose—
to mend and cleanse—make it all His to use.

"Ah! This is the vessel I've been hoping to find.
I will mend it and use it—and make it all Mine!
I need not the vessel with pride of itself;

nor the one so narrow who sits on the shelf.
Not the one who is big-mouthed and shallow and loud;
nor the one that displays its contents so proud.
Not the one who thinks he can do all things just right—
But this plain earthen vessel, filled with My Power and
   Might."

Then gently He lifted the vessel of clay—
mended and cleansed it and filled it that day.
Spoke to it kindly—"There's work you must do.
You pour out to others—and I'll pour into you!"[1]

   As I reread the poem, I couldn't stop the tears for a few minutes. I realized God does not need an attractive vessel to display the budding of his love. A vase should never distract from the beauty of the rose.

   My prayer for myself and my family was that each of our future Christmases would be times of generosity and gentleness. That they would be seasons of gathering together and shutting out the unnecessary things of the world. That we might all choose to slow down and focus on simple acts of sharing who we are and what we have. That our meditations would prepare our hearts for the seasons of the coming year—when we could more fully be flavorful salt and attractive light to those we love and serve. And that people might see our loving work in such a way that they would glorify our Father in heaven.[2]

   I blew my nose and opened my journal to jot a thought:

I've always thought of Christmas as a time for looking back, reflecting on the blessings and lessons of the previous year—to use them as a foundation for next year's growth. Each year's journey is new, never traveled before, yet God makes his light shine in our hearts[3] and gives us his inspired wisdom[4] to serve as a foot lamp for our path[5]—not the entire road ahead, but just enough guidance for our next few steps—leading us each day to believe unshakably, hope unswervingly, and love unwaveringly.

I opened my Bible to the book of Colossians. Finding the verses I was seeking, I jotted them down:

> So, chosen by God for this new life of love, dress in the wardrobe God picked out for you: compassion, kindness, humility, quiet strength, discipline. Be even-tempered, content with second place, quick to forgive an offense. Forgive as quickly and completely as the Master forgave you. And regardless of what else you put on, wear love. It's your basic, all-purpose garment. Never be without it.[6]

I looked up at the dying embers of the fire. I loved the fragrance of the balsam from our tree and the aroma of the burning wood. I got up to add a log. It slowly ignited and began to give off light and warmth.

As I sat back down, it seemed to me the logs burning together was a metaphor for life. My Creator did not design me to, nor can I successfully, navigate my journey through life—its burdens and bliss—without trusted companions. As my road unfolds each year, I've found it foolish to walk alone. Instead, I choose to travel side by side with dependable confidants as we move together from darkness into light—from tragedy into triumph.

I wrote my final thought for the evening:

> When it comes to all Christmas gifts, I think I do best to keep my focus on Jesus. He's the only dependable and trustworthy illumination and enlightenment I've had during all my dark times. He is the promised and ultimate Morning Star who assures me that he will bring lasting light not only to my heart but to the world.[7]

Looking back on my early years as both a family physician and a follower of Jesus, my personal identity was based upon my gifts, talents, achievements, and social standing—my outer ornaments and adornments.

The story I've told you began with the tale of a wreck. It represents my life before Jesus rescued me, the Holy Spirit patched me up and began to heal me, and friends came along to pray and care for me.

You see, God loved me even though I loved me more than he—when I was foolishly choosing my way over Yahweh. He didn't abandon me or give up on me. Rather, he graciously used his Spirit, his Word, and his people to encourage, equip, and enable me to take my first feeble steps on the rather difficult spiritual quest to grasp, hold on to, embrace, and then bear witness to a new identity.

I began to understand the uniqueness, distinctiveness, and necessity of becoming a changed person, a new creature, a man striving to be salt and light for the benefit of his family, friends, colleagues, and patients—for my good and even more so for my Father's glory. An accomplishment only possible through many trials and tribulations, storms and sufferings.

In The Message translation, Pastor Eugene Peterson transliterates something Jesus said to his disciples about what they could expect for themselves: "Anyone who intends to come with me has to let me lead. You're not in the driver's seat; *I* am. Don't run from suffering; embrace it. Follow me and I'll show you how."[8]

Up to that point, I had been a family physician who happened to be a Christian. Now, I was finally on the road to becoming a Christian who happened to be a family physician—one called, privileged, and honored to represent the Great Physician.

I had a long way to go, but hopefully, I was making a good start due to the love, guidance, and empowering of him, the best gift of all.

Acknowledgments

The movie and TV series *Fargo* both begin by saying, "This is a true story," and go on to state, "At the request of the survivors, the names have been changed. Out of respect for the dead, the rest has been told exactly as it occurred."[1]

Similarly, this book is based upon true stories, but the "survivors" are all friends who have consented to have their stories shared with you. I'm thankful to and for Jennifer and Jerry Adamson; Kathy Baker; Wayne, Janet, Lyndsey, and John Cook; John and Cleta Hartman; Bill and Jane Judge; Barb Larimore; Scott Larimore; Susan Mongillo; Jackie Niles; Dawn Pate; Jean Parten; Bill and Polly Prather; Allan Pratt; Alice Ramsey; Scott Ramsey; Don and Pauline Rinkus; Kate Larimore (Ritz); Frank R. Ross; Jimmy Sabetto; Jim Shanks; Tina Rinkus (Sines); Tim and Nancy Wilder; Joanne Woida; Mark, Laura, and Jonathan Zieg; and Pastor Pete and Judy Zieg.

Four other dear friends not only agreed to let me put them in the book but also to represent their professional colleagues: Ken Byerly, MD, for the ER doctors; Hamp Sessions, MD, for the radiologists; Sandi Lynch, RN, for the hospital nurses; and Judy Simpson (Tidball) for the office nurses I worked with for over fifteen years. Other incredibly influential characters mentioned in this book who have passed include Frank Attkisson, Coach Allan Baker, Paul Brand, Pete Gonzales, Harold Epperson, David Larson, Clem McSpadden, Connie and Geech Partin, Cynthia Sabetto, and Don Shearer.

All other characters are composites of one or more real people. Most bear names that are purely fictional—primarily to protect the identity of those the story was based on and secondarily to protect those who are either blameless or grumpy or both. Many times, I've changed the name, gender, and age of people (especially patients) to protect their confidentiality and privacy.

Most of the stories in this book are recorded as they happened or how I remember them happening. Others are adapted from my other writings, including the "Diary of a Week in Practice" column that I wrote from 1992 to 2001 for *American Family Physician*. Still others are drawn from phone or in-person interviews, written communications, and my journal and prayer logs.

A most special thank-you is extended to my dear friends and mentors John Hartman, MD, and Bill Judge. I love them. John and Bill are still my most authentic models of what it means to be Christians who also happen to be a family physician or a farmer.

I want to make a special note about the two poems I quote, which have had a considerable impact on me, not only when I first read them but also over the last three decades.

B. V. Cornwall, a pastor's wife and the author of "The Vessel" (see pages 248–49), has passed away; however, I'm grateful to her only surviving child, Dr. Iverna M. Tompkins (Iverna Tompkins Ministries International), for permitting me to share the poem with you. If you choose to reproduce it, please quote it accurately (with no edits or deletions) and indicate it by © B. V. Cornwall. Should you feel moved to contribute to Dr. Tompkins's ministry in her mother's name, this can be done online at IvernaInternational .com.

Claudia Minden Weisz, author of "And God Said 'No'" (see

page 128), tells me she wrote this heartfelt lament as a psalm to God as she cared for Angela, her precious daughter, who suffered from Rett syndrome—even before this terrible disorder had a name. Angela graduated to glory at forty-two years of age. Although Claudia's original poem is copyrighted, countless people worldwide have altered and published it without her permission— many without even crediting Claudia. Others have profited from her poem without sharing any of their ill-earned profits with her.

I'm grateful to Claudia for permitting me to use the original version of her poem. She says, "It was freely given to me by God, and others are free to use it also." Her only request: "If the poem touches you, go out and love someone else today, by action or a charitable contribution." And if you reproduce it, quote it accurately (with no edits or deletions) and indicate it by © Claudia Minden Weisz (1980). Also should you feel moved to contribute to RettSyndrome.org in Angela Weisz's name, this can be done online.

I'm again grateful for the superb editing skills of Cindy Lambert, Vicki Crumpton, and especially Robin Turici. I appreciate the team at Revell for their remarkable assistance. Special thanks are due to Sarah Asprec, Scott Bolinder, Laura Klynstra, Mark Rice, Kelli Smith, Sarah Traill, and Wendy Wetzel. Thanks also to Greg Johnson, the founder and president of WordServe Literary Agency, who represents me and has become a trusted friend. I appreciate Don Jones of Studio 9 Commercial Photography for allowing me to use a portrait he took of me. You can see his fantastic work at tinyurl.com/nufrxwmu.

A special thanks is due to Amy Odland (AmyOdland.com), who as Book Launch Team Manager, facilitated the very active and quite successful internet launch teams for both *The Best Medicine* and this book. Thanks, Amy!

I loved working with my friend (and coauthor with me on *God's Design for the Highly Healthy Teen* and *At First Light: A True World War II Story of a Hero and His Horse*), Mike Yorkey, on the book's final draft. It reads so much better with the application of Mike's superb edits and suggestions. I'm also thankful for Sherry Compton (former rodeo barrel racer and media manager for the ProRodeo Cowboys Association), Steve Dail (horseman and cowboy), as well as Barb Larimore, Lois Johnson Rew (author of *Editing for Writers*[2]), and Katherine Larimore Ritz, for reading early drafts of the manuscript and providing excellent suggestions. I appreciate Anza Bast, one of the archives assistants at the Osceola County Historical Society, for providing a fact check for the historical portions of the book, and the *Orlando Sentinel* for providing its archives for my review.

My forty books have all been reviewed and approved by the elders at my local church. For this one, I owe a debt of gratitude to the elders at Academy Christian Church in Colorado Springs. Thanks to Jim Collier, MD, Pastor Richard Crabtree, Al Fritts, and Dave Smith for their review and insightful comments.

A most sincere and joyous thanks to Kate, Scott, and Barb—my wife-for-life and very bestest friend—for their endless love and support and for allowing me to share their stories with you.

Walt Larimore, MD
Colorado Springs
July 2021

Other Resources from Walt Larimore, MD

Health Books

The Natural Medicine Handbook: The Truth about the Most Effective Herbs, Vitamins, and Supplements for Common Conditions

Alternative Medicine: The Options, the Claims, the Evidence, How to Choose Wisely (with Dónal O'Mathúna)

Fit over 50: Make Simple Choices Today for a Healthier, Happier You (with Phillip Bishop)

God's Design for the Highly Healthy Child (with Stephen and Amanda Sorenson)

God's Design for the Highly Healthy Person (with Traci Mullins)

God's Design for the Highly Healthy Teen (with Mike Yorkey)

The Highly Healthy Child (with Traci Mullins)

Lintball Leo's Not-So-Stupid Questions about Your Body (with John Riddle)

SuperSized Kids: How to Rescue Your Child from the Obesity Threat (with Sherri Flynt and Steve Halliday)

10 Essentials of Highly Healthy People: Becoming and Staying Highly Healthy

The Ultimate Girls' Body Book: Not-So-Silly Questions about Your Body (with Amaryllis Sánchez Wohlever)

The Ultimate Guys' Body Book: Not-So-Stupid Questions about Your Body

Why ADHD Doesn't Mean Disaster (with Dennis Swanburg and Diane Passno)

Memoirs from My Practice

The Best Medicine: Tales of Humor and Hope from a Small-Town Doctor

Bryson City Tales: Stories of a Doctor's First Year of Practice in the Smoky Mountains

Bryson City Seasons: More Tales of a Doctor's Practice in the Smoky Mountains

Bryson City Secrets: Even More Tales of a Small-Town Doctor in the Smoky Mountains

Web Resources

www.DrWalt.com

www.DrWalt.com/Blog

www.Devotional.DrWalt.com

Notes

All URLs were last accessed on May 7, 2021.

Epigraph

1. Luke 9:2 BBE.

Chapter 3 It's Hot Here

1. For this chapter, I refreshed my memory with the following: (1) an interview with Geech and Connie's daughter, Kathy Baker, in October 2019; (2) Jovida Fletcher, "Coming of Age in Osceola in the '50s Meant a Lot of Freedom," *Orlando Sentinel*, June 3, 1990, tinyurl.com/y53lgplm (subscription required); (3) "History of Kissimmee," Osceola County, tinyurl.com/yy3gw9z2; (4) Larry Manfredi, *Birds of Central Florida: A Guide to Common and Notable Species*, pamphlet ed. (Ft. Lauderdale, FL: Quick Reference Publishing, Inc., 2009); and (5) "One Town's Origins: The History of Kissimmee," Osceola County Historical Society, tinyurl.com/53m485hn.

Chapter 5 Expect the Unexpected

1. *Well come* is a phrase describing the person that means "happily arrived" or "safely appearing."

Chapter 6 Discipler

1. 2 Timothy 3:12 MSG.
2. Job 23:10.
3. 1 Peter 4:12 NLT.
4. Rev. H. K. Williams, "The Group Plan," in *Biblical World* (Chicago: University of Chicago Press, 1919), 53:81, tinyurl.com/dn2c4ycy.
5. Matthew 24:42.

6. Luke 21:36 NLT.
7. James 1:2–4.
8. Proverbs 10:25.
9. 1 Peter 4:13 CEV.
10. Romans 8:18 CEV.

Chapter 7 Imminent Calamity

1. For this chapter, I refreshed my memory by interviewing Sandi Lynch, RN; Allan Pratt, DO; Laura Zieg; Mark Zieg; and Pete Zieg.

Chapter 8 Baptism under Fire

1. Psalm 40:17 CSB.
2. Personal communication from Pete Zieg, May 28, 2020. For this chapter, I refreshed my memory by interviewing Sandi Lynch, RN; Allan Pratt, DO; Laura Zieg; Mark Zieg; and Pete Zieg.

Chapter 9 Rodeo Time

1. Burkhard Bilger, "The Ride of Their Lives: Children Prepare for the World's Most Dangerous Organized Sport," *The New Yorker*, December 8, 2014, tinyurl.com/yyp4kz2b.
2. For this chapter, I refreshed my memory with the following: (1) an interview with Geech and Connie's daughter, Kathy Baker; (2) "Silver Spurs Rodeo History," Silver Spurs Rodeo, tinyurl.com/y6nlsus9.

Chapter 10 Don't Lose the Lesson

1. For this chapter, I refreshed my memory with the following: (1) an interview with Geech and Connie's daughter, Kathy Baker; (2) "Silver Spurs Rodeo History."

Chapter 11 Quality Time

1. Proverbs 6:16–17.
2. Matthew 5:8 MSG.

Chapter 12 House Fire

1. R. W. Livingstone, ed., *The Pageant of Greece* (London, England: Oxford University Press, 1924), 208.

Chapter 13 A New Trick

1. Mark 10:14–15 NLT.
2. Matthew 18:5 NLT.

Chapter 14 Table Fellowship

1. Romans 5:8; 1 Corinthians 15:3–6; John 14:6.
2. Revelation 3:20 MSG.

3. "Great Minds Discuss Ideas; Average Minds Discuss Events; Small Minds Discuss People," Quote Investigator, tinyurl.com/tdhrdde.

4. Matthew 11:19; Luke 7:34.

5. Matthew 18:20.

6. Matthew 26:29.

7. Isaiah 25:6.

Chapter 15 Faith and Medicine

1. Colossians 3:23.

2. Jennifer Fandel, *Martin Luther King: Genius* (Mankato, MN: Creative Education, 2006), 39.

3. Paul Brand, "The Challenge of Evangelism for the Medical & Dental Professionals," in Leonard W. Ritzman, *Evangelism for the Medical and Dental Professions* (Dallas, TX: Christian Medical and Dental Society, 1990), 19.

4. 1 Thessalonians 5:16–19.

5. James 1:2–4 MSG.

Chapter 16 Life-Giving Hope

1. 1 Thessalonians 1:3.

2. Proverbs 13:12 NLT.

3. Menachem Feuer, "He Gave Him Another Six Months: Comedy, Economics, and Dream Interpretation in Henny Youngman and the Talmud," Schlemiel Theory, March 2, 2014, tinyurl.com/dn2c4ycy.

4. Proverbs 13:12 MSG.

Chapter 17 Born Again and Again

1. 1 John 5:12–13.

2. John 3:3, 6–7.

3. John 1:12–13.

4. 1 John 5:13.

Chapter 18 The Missing Link

1. 1 Corinthians 3:6–7.

2. John 6:44–46 MSG.

3. Colossians 4:5.

4. Colossians 4:6.

5. John 4:7.

6. Luke 1:9.

7. Luke 2:8.

8. Matthew 4:21.

9. Luke 5:27.

10. Exodus 15:26 ESV.

11. Isaiah 57:19.

12. Jeremiah 30:17 ISV.

Chapter 19 God Said "No"

1. Claudia provided the 1980 copyrighted text and granted permission for the use of her poem.

Chapter 20 Where Y'at?

1. This quote may be derived from Moses Maimonides (Ramban), Less Is More Medicine, tinyurl.com/ybsklkuu.
2. Attributed to "Old Dr. Parry of Bath . . . a Century Ago," in James Joseph Walsh, *Psychotherapy* (New York: D. Appleton and Company, 1912), 160; Quote Investigator, tinyurl.com/y9tmuwas.

Chapter 21 Margie

1. J. Sidlow Baxter, quoted in Charlie Jones and Bob Kelly, *The Tremendous Power of Prayer* (West Monroe, LA: Howard Publishing, 2000), 46.

Chapter 22 Leon

1. Genesis 2:7.
2. Genesis 2:18.

Chapter 23 Patients and Friends

1. 2 Corinthians 5:17 NLT.
2. John 10:10; Psalm 16:11; Galatians 5:22–23.

Chapter 24 Amazing Bull

1. Dave Trimmer, "Perfection Reflection Wade Leslie's 8-Second, 100-Point Bull Ride Will be Remembered as Best in PRCA History," *The Spokesman-Review*, February 3, 1995, tinyurl.com/y6ppluhp.
2. "Good Judgment Depends Mostly on Experience and Experience Usually Comes from Poor Judgment," Quote Investigator, tinyurl.com/y724majw.
3. For this chapter, I refreshed my memory with the following: (1) an interview with Geech and Connie's daughter, Kathy Baker; (2) Jovida Fletcher, "Legend of Cowboy Jake Survives Change," *Orlando Sentinel*, June 29, 1991; (3) Katrina Elsken, "Day of the Cowboy Rodeo Honors Iconic Cowboy," *Lake Okeechobee News*, July 24, 2019; and (4) "Silver Spurs Rodeo History."

Chapter 25 Memorable Auctions

1. Proverbs 26:11 NLT.

Chapter 28 Code Blue, ICU

1. "It Is Well with My Soul," Wikipedia, tinyurl.com/ycwvo3b2.
2. Horatio Gates Spafford and Philip Bliss (1876). "When Peace Like a River,"

Lutheran Book of Worship: 346, Public Domain Hymns, Luther Seminary, tinyurl
.com/3epccd2f.

3. Matthew 10:37 NLT.

4. T. S. Eliot, "Bustopher Jones: The Cat about Town," in *Old Possum's Book of Practical Cats* (London, England: Faber and Faber, 1939).

Chapter 29 The Prank

1. 1 John 1:9 ESV.

Chapter 30 The Unkindest Cut

1. Mark E. Silverman, T. Jock Murray, and Charles S. Bryan, *The Quotable Osler* (Philadelphia: The American College of Physicians, 2008), 85, tinyurl.com/y7f6u2qa.

2. "Treating Self or Family," American Medical Association, tinyurl.com/y5lfynuz.

3. Joseph Herbert Larimore, *James and Susannah (Bonheim) Larimore Family History* (self-published, year unknown), 1–3. The original is held in the library of the Licking County Genealogical Society in Newark, Ohio. The author writes that his account "is drawn largely from a history of the Larimore family written by Caroline Larimore Williams of Wheeling, W. Va."

Chapter 31 By-and-By

1. Proverbs 17:22 GNT.

2. Clem McSpadden, "The Cowboy's Prayer," Cowboy Way, tinyurl.com/yyhdeao2.

3. Psalm 113:3.

4. Ecclesiastes 7:3 NLT.

5. James 1:2–4 MSG.

6. For this chapter, I refreshed my memory with the following: (1) an interview with Geech and Connie's daughter, Kathy Baker; (2) Jovida Fletcher, "Geech Partin's Legacy Now Includes 'Hall of Famer,'" *Orlando Sentinel*, March 3, 1996, tinyurl.com/y8rv9n8m (subscription required); (3) "Florida Cattle Ranching," Florida Memory, tinyurl.com/y62vl63x; (4) Rowland Stiteler, "The Last of the Cowboys: Geech Partin and the Partin Clan," *Orlando Sentinel*, November 23, 1986, tinyurl.com/yywpg96o (subscription required).

Chapter 32 Lady in Red

1. Dr. Seuss, *Horton Hears a Who!* (New York: Random House, 1954), 7.

2. Lakeside Inn website, tinyurl.com/yddqmlhg.

3. Lakeside Inn website.

4. Jeremiah 31:13 NLT.

5. 2 Kings 20:5.

6. Psalm 34:18.

7. Psalm 27:10 NLT.

8. Luke 6:21 ESV.
9. Jeremiah 14:17 MSG.
10. Psalm 34:18 NLT.
11. Psalm 34:18 MSG.
12. Jeremiah 8:19.
13. Zephaniah 3:17; Isaiah 62:5.
14. Psalm 103:8; Joel 2:13.
15. Genesis 6:6; Psalm 78:40.
16. Isaiah 63:10; Psalm 78:40.
17. 1 John 4:8.
18. For this chapter, I refreshed my memory with the following: (1) an interview with Geech and Connie's daughter, Kathy Baker; (2) Fletcher, "Geech Partin's Legacy"; (3) "Florida Cattle Ranching"; (4) Stiteler, "The Last of the Cowboys."

Chapter 33 Misery to Ministry

1. 2 Samuel 12:15–23 ESV.
2. Jeremiah 1:5.
3. Psalm 51:5.
4. J. Vernon McGee, *Death of a Little Child* (Pasadena, CA: Thru the Bible Radio, 1970), 20.

Chapter 35 Night of Tornadoes

1. Mike Oliver, "Looking Back: The Deadliest Night of Tornadoes in Florida History," *Orlando Sentinel*, February 23, 2014, tinyurl.com/yy9z3zyn (subscription required).
2. For this chapter, I refreshed my memory with the following: (1) Amanda Holly, "Why Florida Is Lightning Capital of US," WFLA, July 23, 2019, tinyurl.com/y5m67d69; (2) Kimberly Miller, "Florida's 10 Safest Cities in a Hurricane," *Palm Beach Post*, July 9, 2018, tinyurl.com/y6tcv868; (3) "Lightning More Dangerous Than Tornadoes or Hurricanes," Naples News, June 12, 2007, tinyurl.com/yy6tg493; (4) "List of Florida Hurricanes," Wikipedia, tinyurl.com/jgj86gy; (5) Stephen Nohlgren and Wilma Norton, "'The Sound of Death': Deadly Tornadoes Ravage Central Florida in Dark (from 1998)," *Tampa Bay Times*, February 23, 2018, tinyurl.com/y3tsbjzl; (6) Oliver, "Looking Back"; and (7) "Study: Florida #1 in Tornadoes and Deaths," *Brevard Times*, June 16, 2014, tinyurl.com/y5xs9xga.

Chapter 36 Haunting Silence

1. Susan Lewis, "The Story behind the Beloved Christmas Carol 'Silent Night'," wrti90.1, tinyurl.com/y294j87o. With lyrics by Joseph Mohr and melody by Franz Xaver Gruber, "Silent Night, Holy Night [Stille Nacht, Heilige Nacht]" was first publicly performed at the Christmas Eve Mass in 1818 at the St. Nicholas Church in Oberndorf, Germany. It was declared an intangible cultural heritage by UNESCO in 2011.
2. For this chapter, I refreshed my memory with the following: (1) Nohlgren and Norton, "The Sound of Death"; (2) Oliver, "Looking Back."

Chapter 38 A True Miracle

1. Wess Stafford and Dean Merrill, *Too Small to Ignore: Why the Least of These Matters Most* (Colorado Springs: Waterbrook Press, 2007), 207.

Chapter 39 Not Our Final Home

1. "Storm Events Database," NOAA, tinyurl.com/y3zkdqwk.
2. Job 42:2–3 NLT.
3. C. S. Lewis, *The Problem of Pain* (London: Geoffrey Bles, 1940), 81.
4. Romans 8:28 CEV.
5. Revelation 21:3–4.

Chapter 40 Fear Not

1. Luke 2:1–16.
2. Luke 2:10 NASB.
3. Luke 2:10–11 NASB.
4. Luke 2:10–11 CSB.
5. For this chapter, I refreshed my memory by having Pastors Tim Wilder and Pete Zieg review their quotes.

Chapter 41 The Best Gift

1. Lewis, "Story behind the Beloved Christmas Carol," tinyurl.com/j7omts4.
2. "Joy to the World" was first published in 1719 by Isaac Watts. It was based on Psalm 98, Psalm 96:11–12, and Genesis 3:17–18. It is the most-published Christmas hymn in North America, tinyurl.com/y2rfv36g.

Epilogue

1. B. V. Cornwall, "The Vessel," quoted by her daughter, Dr. Iverna M. Tompkins, "The Peninnah Syndrome," transcribed by Jane Vaughn, Iverna International, tinyurl.com/p632p37u. Used with permission.
2. Matthew 5:13–16.
3. 2 Corinthians 4:6.
4. 2 Timothy 3:16–17.
5. Psalm 119:105.
6. Colossians 3:12–14 MSG.
7. 2 Peter 1:16–21 MSG.
8. Matthew 16:24–25 MSG.

Acknowledgments

1. "Was 'Fargo' Based on a True Story?" Snopes, June 9, 1988, tinyurl.com /y4yru69n.
2. Lois Johnson Rew, *Editing for Writers* (New York: Pearson, 1998).

Walt Larimore, MD, has been a family physician for forty years, and he still enjoys caring for patients in the office setting. He's an award-winning and bestselling author, known for his Bryson City books, *The Best Medicine*, and *The Natural Medicine Handbook*. Dr. Walt is a prolific author of forty books, thirty medical textbook chapters, and over one thousand articles in a wide variety of medical journals and lay magazines; has been called "one of America's best-known family physicians;" and was the recipient of a lifetime achievement award from Marquis Who's Who in 2019. He has been listed in the *Best Doctors in America*, *Distinguished Physicians of America*, *Who's Who in Medicine and Healthcare*, *Who's Who in America*, *Who's Who in the World*, and the *International Health Professionals of the Year*. He writes a bimonthly health column, "Ask Dr. Walt," for *Today's Christian Living* magazine and hosts *Ask Dr. Walt* on Liftable TV. Dr. Walt also writes a daily blog called "Medical News You Can Use," which you can subscribe to at www.DrWalt.com/blog. And he pens a twice-daily biblical devotion called "Morning Glory, Evening Grace," which you can subscribe to at www.Devotional.DrWalt.com. Both are free. For three decades, Dr. Walt has been a frequent guest talking about family health topics on a wide variety of television and radio shows. He and his wife love serving in their local church, hiking and gardening, and maybe most of all, being grandparents. They currently live in Colorado Springs, Colorado.

CONNECT WITH DR. WALT

To learn more about Walt Larimore, MD, and read his blogs, visit

DRWALT.COM

EVIDENCE-BASED ADVICE
YOU CAN TRUST

Return to nature's medicine with *The Natural Medicine Handbook*. Find natural interventions for almost 500 common conditions, arranged topically. Featuring many helpful charts and tables, this reliable guide will tell you what natural medicines have proven to be both safe and effective.

An Honest and Heartwarming
Journey of Discovery

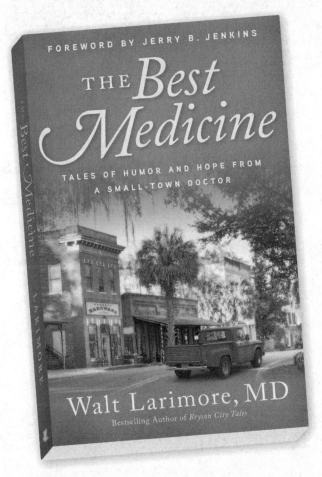

This tender, insightful collection of stories chronicles
Dr. Walt's passage from inexperience to maturity as a
physician, husband, father, and community member.
Filled with winsome characters, these captivating stories
glow with warmth, love, and humor. You'll laugh, you'll cry,
and you'll wish Dr. Walt was your doctor.